MARRIAGE 911

marriage
911

How
God Saved
Our Marriage
(and can save yours, too!)

. . . .

GREG AND JULIE ALEXANDER

FOREWORD BY CURTIS AND MICHAELANN MARTIN

SERVANT
BOOKS

PUBLISHED BY FRANCISCAN MEDIA
Cincinnati, Ohio

Unless otherwise noted, Scripture passages have been taken from the *Revised Standard Version*, Catholic edition. Copyright 1946, 1952, 1971 by the Division of Christian Education of the National Council of Churches of Christ in the USA. Used by permission. All rights reserved. Scripture passages marked *NAB* are from *The New American Bible with Revised New Testament and Revised Psalms* © 1991, 1986, 1970 Confraternity of Christian Doctrine, Washington, D.C. and are used by permission of the copyright owner. All Rights Reserved. No part of the *New American Bible* may be reproduced in any form without permission in writing from the copyright owner.

Cover and book design by Mark Sullivan
Cover image © Infinity | Veer

LIBRARY OF CONGRESS CATALOGING-IN-PUBLICATION DATA
Alexander, Greg.
Marriage 911 : how God saved our marriage (and can save yours, too) / Greg and Julie Alexander.
p. cm.
Includes bibliographical references and index.
ISBN 978-0-86716-979-9 (alk. paper)
1. Marriage—Religious aspects—Catholic Church. 2. Alexander, Greg. 3. Alexander, Julie. I. Alexander, Julie. II. Title.
BX2250.A5375 2011
248.8'440922—dc22
[B]
2011014623

ISBN 978-0-86716-979-9

Copyright © 2011, Greg and Julie Alexander. All rights reserved.
Published by Servant Books,
an imprint of Franciscan Media
28 W. Liberty St.
Cincinnati, OH 45202
www.FranciscanMedia.org

Printed in the United States of America.
Printed on acid-free paper.
14 15   5 4 3

Contents

Foreword

IMAGINE FOR A MOMENT A typical wedding day: a young couple in love, months of planning filled with hope and dreams—and all too often a share of tension over the details. All the planning and arrangements started with the simple desire, one man and one woman want to spend the rest of their lives together; they fell in love and want to live "happily ever after." In fact, when we think of a wedding, it is hard to imagine a young couple coming together with anything *but* love, hope for the future, and the desire to make each other's life better. That's what marriage is all about. Isn't it?

So how did things go so badly?

Despite the best of intentions, far too many marriages end in divorce, and even the marriages that "stay together" seem to fall far short of wedding day hopes. Couples, who only a short time ago wanted to share their lives with one another, have become satisfied with merely sharing a mailing address. We have a problem. Have you noticed? All is not as it ought to be. Something seems to have gone terribly wrong. Marriage is in a state of emergency. Someone needs to call 911, and that is precisely what Greg and Julie Alexander have done.

There is a simple principle in life: If you aim at nothing, you will hit it every time. So, yes, we need to know what we are aiming for. The target is not merely avoiding divorce, or even to trying to stay friends. God's goal for our married lives is that we love each other more as time goes on and that we, together, love him more because of our marriage.

To build a healthy marriage, good intentions and sincerity are absolutely essential, but they are not enough. Think of a master builder who desires to build a bridge across a mighty river but is working with a flawed blueprint. Each day he comes to work with the sincere desire to build the best bridge he possibly can. Weeks pass, and then months; the bridge is taking shape, but despite the best efforts of a devoted team, the project is riddled with complications. The problem is in the blueprint. No matter how hard you work or how great the materials are that you have to work with, if your blueprint is defective, your efforts will fail. Marriage is like that bridge; fortunately Greg and Julie discovered the Master's blueprint for marriage—the teachings of the Catholic Church.

Discovering God's plans for marriage and family is just the first step. We have been blessed with a great marriage; we discovered God's blueprint for married love early, and we have tried to live our lives accordingly. We have been able to avoid some of the major pitfalls that ensnare so many couples, and we thank God for that. You would think that with God's design for marriage clear in our minds, it would make marriage *easy*. It doesn't—it merely makes marriage *possible*. A holy and happy marriage takes more; we need help from the outside. And that is precisely what God desires to give us: his grace. Despite my desire to love Michaelann, and despite my desire to respect Curtis, through life we each fall short and fail to live up to our best intentions, every day. We find that even when we know what we are aiming for, we stumble. On our own we simply do not have what it takes to keep the vows we made to one another—but we are not on our own.

This is where's God's plan for marriage gets really exciting. He doesn't just sit on the sidelines cheering for us; he joins our team. In order to live his plan, we need God's help, his very life, his love, and his mercy—in a word, we need his grace. Equipped, with God's plan and with God's grace, we can add our sincere desire and commitment and choose to experience all of the joy and richness God has waiting for us.

Greg and Julie have an amazing story. It has been the source of blessing to countless couples, and we stand in awe at the wonderful work of the Alexander House, which has helped so many couples find the joy they longed for on the their wedding day. Greg and Julie have done us a great favor—now, do yourself a favor and read this book. In the midst of their own marriage, tested to the very limits of what you can imagine, they made a choice, a choice you can make right now. They will show you how to turn towards God to receive the desire to begin again. You may think your marriage is hopeless, or even dead, but we have a God who has risen from the dead and he lives to share his life with you. You may think things are as bad as they can get—so make the call, turn the page, and begin *Marriage 911*.

—*Curtis and Michaelann Martin*

Preface

IF YOU'RE READING THIS BOOK just because you want to hear our story and you want to know more about what we do, then go right ahead. Have fun. We hope you'll be inspired, and maybe even entertained.

But if you think your marriage is in need of attention, and you're hoping this book will help, then we want you to answer three questions.

1. Is this marriage relationship something you want, and is it something you're willing to work on, and will you do the things we prescribe for you to do?
2. Do you have the faith that Jesus Christ has the ability and the power to redeem your marriage and restore it to where it needs to be?
3. Do you give God the permission to come into your life and to redeem it?

Consider these questions very carefully. These are the same questions we ask when couples come to us privately for coaching. And if you can honestly answer yes to all three, then we think we can help you get your marriage back on track.

We Need a Divorce

I REMEMBER THE MOMENT I knew our marriage was healed. We were driving home from confession, and Greg and I both felt as if a huge weight had been lifted from us.

"It's like all the stuff we did to each other is gone," Greg said. "I've totally forgiven you. It's gone."

I looked at him. He was smiling. And I knew exactly how he felt, because I felt the same way about him. This was the man I loved—the man I'd always loved.

I didn't always think he was the man I loved. We'd been through a lot, and we'd done things to each other that I was ready to say were unforgivable.

But there was a way out, and we found it. If we tell you how rotten we were to each other, it's not because we like to wallow in misery. It's because we want you to know that you can get from there to here.

*   *   *

I think the day we hit rock bottom was the day that my friend showed up at the door with her brother. Greg answered the door, and she told him she had a belated Christmas present for me. So Greg called me down, and that was when she tore into me.

"How long have you and my husband been having an affair?"

She went on from there for about half an hour. She fired off questions, accusations, demands. Greg just stood by and watched. I didn't get a word in edgewise.

And anyway, what could I say? It was all true.

After she had made it clear in every way she could think of that I wasn't going to go near her husband again, she finally left. I just sat there.

Greg finally broke the silence. "How could you?" he asked quietly.

All I could think of to say was, "Well, our marriage hasn't been real good anyway."

He asked a few more questions, and I didn't have much more to say. But then he said something that still managed to shock me: "I can't be too upset with you, because I had an affair too."

What? How could he cheat on me? Who did he think he was?

Yes, I was hurt and upset. And I was furious. It was irrational and selfish and unfair, I know. He hadn't been any worse than I'd been. But *his* doing it to *me* was different from *my* doing it to *him!*

Finally Greg pretty much summed up the past two years of our marriage: "You're unhappy, and I'm unhappy. Why don't we just get a divorce?"

"Fine," I said, and that was it.

It made perfect sense. I certainly didn't want to be with him anymore—not after what he'd done to me. (Funny how quickly that canceled out what I'd done to him.) I was in the marriage for what Greg could bring to the marriage. He wasn't bringing anything to the marriage for me anymore, so I was done. It was time to recognize that our marriage wasn't working and call it quits. Wasn't that the honest thing to do?

But of course there was one complication. We'd have to tell the kids.

I think Greg was using "telling the kids" as a test to see how serious I was about going through with the divorce. I guess he was hoping I'd change my mind and decide I wanted to work on our marriage. He even threatened that he would take the kids when we were divorced. After all, he'd been taking care of them most of the time while I was out building up my career.

I certainly didn't want to lose contact with my kids. But I didn't want to work on the marriage either. I was just worn out. "There's no possible way out of this," I told myself. "Even if we did stay together, there's no way I could ever feel love for him again."

I couldn't understand how it had happened. I had stood at the altar with this man and said, "I do." But now if he walked past me and touched me, I wanted to throw up. I felt chilled on the inside.

That's how we were living our lives. We were married, yes, but we didn't have anything in common. I mean, we had a house together; we had kids together; we even had a joint checking account. But we were spiritually divorced. We had nothing in common that brought us together on a daily basis.

So after a couple of days, I told Greg he could tell the kids. I didn't know how that would go, but we decided to go ahead and do it. Even today I shudder at the thought.

Greg called Christopher and Lauren out of their bedrooms and brought them into ours. I just stood there, numb. It was up to Greg to do the talking. The kids were eight and nine years old at the time, so he tried to explain it in a way they could understand. He crouched down so he was at eye level with them.

"Moms and dads sometimes don't get along, like brothers and sisters," he said. "That's where your mom and I are at right now, so we're going to get a divorce." That was all. Quick and to the point.

The kids started crying. They huddled together, clinging to each other in the corner and pleading, "No, no, no," shaking from the fact that their lives were being ripped apart.

But our hearts were cold. All I could say to myself was *They'll be fine. We'll just send them to counseling. That's what Bob and Sue did down the street, and their kids seem to be OK.*

That's how far gone we were.

*   *   *

But we weren't completely lost, and I think that the experience of telling Christopher and Lauren we were going to get a divorce sort of woke us up. Their reaction was the sobering reality that made us decide that we had to do everything we could to keep our marriage together. Even if we didn't think it could possibly work, we owed it to the kids. We never wanted to look back with any regrets and say that we didn't try everything to make our marriage work.

It wasn't easy. Some days I had hope and wanted to work on the marriage—those were the days Greg wanted nothing to do with it. Other days Greg was really trying hard, and I had no energy to try anymore.

One day my boss walked in on me at work and found me crying. I'd been crying plenty of other times at work, but this was the first time he'd seen me do it. When I was finally able to explain what was going on, he offered to have his girlfriend talk with us. She was a counselor at a prison—not exactly an expert in marriage issues but still a professional.

I took him up on the offer, and Greg and I went to see this counselor. I thought she was OK, but Greg was just getting angry at the questions she asked. We met a few times, but although she had a good heart, we didn't seem to accomplish much.

The last time we met, she told us, "There's going to be a day when you're standing in front of a ton of people telling your story."

Yeah, right, we thought.

*   *   *

We weren't getting anywhere. I remember a day in February when my parents called. I couldn't even muster the courage to talk to them. Greg had to do all the talking, while I just tucked myself into a ball on the bedroom floor.

My parents had the perfect marriage, or at least that's how it seemed to me. Everyone at church knew them from their pro-life work, and everyone respected them. As a daughter, I felt like a failure.

Then Greg came in and put the phone to my ear, and I heard my mother's voice:

"We love you, and we're praying for you."

That was all she said. No judgment, no finger pointing. Just love and support.

* * *

By April I was desperate. I finally picked up the phone and made a 911 call to the pastor of our church. If you're keeping score, you'll notice that this was the first time we thought of somehow involving the church with our problems.

I didn't really want him to answer his phone. I didn't know what I'd say. I was relieved when he didn't pick up, and I could just leave a message.

But my message must have sounded desperate. "We're in trouble, Father!" I blurted into the phone. "We're getting a divorce. Greg wants a divorce. You need to help us!"

Of course, when he heard that on his machine, he called right back and told us to come see him.

We did, but once again we didn't seem to get anywhere. The priest tried his best, but he just didn't know what to do with us. After watching us fight in front of him, he finally asked us—as nicely as he could—"Do you *want* to save your marriage?"

"Do we *want* to save this marriage?" I repeated. I just looked at him and answered, "Not *this* marriage."

"Well, I don't know what to do for you," he answered.

That was sort of a shock. Without really thinking about it, I suppose I'd just imagined that he was somehow going to tell us what to do. I don't remember what I said to him, but it was something like, "You don't understand! Our marriage is miserable. What are *you* going to do about it?"

"*I* can't do anything about it," he answered. "It's up to you two."

It was obvious that our problems were way beyond what he could fix. But he did give us the card of someone who described himself as a Catholic counselor. We left the priest's office still arguing.

*   *   *

Greg and I kept fighting all the way home. I wanted to try the counselor. He didn't want anything to do with the counselor. He was a man, and he didn't need someone else telling him how to live his marriage. But in spite of Greg's unwillingness, I made another desperate phone call, this time to the counselor. "You've got to help us!" I pleaded.

I finally managed to persuade Greg to see the counselor, and we patiently explained our problems to him. Well, probably not so patiently. We probably interrupted each other a lot, and I'm sure each of us blamed the other for most of the problems. But all we got from the counselor was a forty-five-minute lesson in nineteenth-century history.

"Your marriage is like the Civil War," he said after he'd listened to us for the better part of an hour. "Greg is like the North. You're like the South. Maybe you just weren't meant to be together. Oh, and that'll be a hundred dollars. I have my next appointment waiting for me outside. Let's schedule another meeting in two weeks."

But we were thinking, *What do we need an appointment for? You just told us what we'd been waiting to hear!* Our *Catholic* counselor had just validated everything we'd been feeling. We weren't meant to be together. We both walked out of his office thinking, *That's the problem. I married the wrong person.*

Despite the fact that we heard what we thought we wanted to hear, we continued to coexist in the house. Like the proverbial two ships passing in the night. We didn't do or say much to each other. We were just there.

*   *   *

But by God's grace we kept going to church—only because I didn't want my parents to find out I wasn't going. I didn't want to disappoint them. But God works with what we give him, and that was how we met a priest who could help us.

Our pastor went away for the summer for continued studies, and another priest was assigned to our parish. We really liked this new priest: He had a wonderful gift for explaining the faith in a way that really made it come alive. I mean, we would be literally on the edges of our seats, and we couldn't wait to go back the next Sunday. So we started hanging out between the two Masses to find out who this guy was and to get to know him. After several weeks we found out that he was the tribunal vicar for the diocese.

Now, if we knew nothing else about our faith, we knew that this was the guy who did that annulment thing. What a gift from God! Here we were, wondering what to do with ourselves, and God had just sent us this holy man to help us get out of our miserable marriage! God was better than we had ever imagined him to be!

I called in one of my desperate moments and said, "Father, could we come see you?"

He said, "Sure, come on by."

The poor man had no idea what was coming when we made an appointment to see him. He thought we were coming for a social visit. Instead, when we got to his office, he had to sit and listen to our story of misery while we pleaded our case as to why we could not stay married. He had to be a godly man, because for forty-five minutes straight he sat there patiently while I told him what a miserable husband Greg was, and Greg told him how I focused on everything but him. "He's done this," "She's done that."

When we finally took a breath long enough for him to speak, he looked at us very gently across the desk and said, "I understand you've been through a lot."

Well, that was an understatement, I thought. But at least he understood.

"But let me ask you a few questions," he continued. "What is God's plan for marriage? What does our Church teach about the marriage covenant? What do the holy fathers and St. Paul say about marriage?"

I just stared at him. I didn't know what to answer. I looked at Greg, and he shrugged his shoulders. It was obvious that he didn't know either.

"Father," I said at last, "what does that have to do with us? I mean, we're Catholic, we go to church on Sundays, but this is our marriage we're talking about. We used to be in love, and now we're not anymore. We were just hoping *you* could show us how to get out of this thing."

"I know it doesn't make sense," he answered, "but before you go any further, I want you to go learn about God's plan for marriage."

We walked out of his office completely confused. "Well," I said to Greg as we pulled away from the parking lot, "that didn't go the way we expected."

We had thought we'd get an easy annulment and move on with our lives. After all, if ever there was a marriage that wasn't working, it was ours. We were both miserable; we'd both been unfaithful and caused each other so much hurt and pain. We thought God had sent us this priest to show us an easy way out.

Instead we were given an assignment: We'd have to learn what God really wanted from us in marriage. We'd have to read the Bible. (Did we even know where our Bible was?)

And once we'd done that, we'd have to look back to the beginning of our relationship and figure out what we'd done wrong. But I think I'll let Greg tell that part of the story. He can start from the beginning.

Before you go on...
Ask yourself a few questions:
• If you have relationship problems, where do you go for help?
• When you look at Church teachings, are you honestly trying to find out what the Church teaches? Or are you looking for something that will confirm your own personal beliefs and prejudices?

In the Beginning

I STOOD IN THE CAFETERIA at St. Edward's University listening to my friend Joanna tell me all about freshman orientation and how much fun she was having. I was getting impatient as she talked, because two weeks earlier we had run into each other at the mall in Houston, and she had said she would introduce me to her roommate at school. I remembered her saying she thought we might hit it off, and that's all I could think about as she spoke.

"That's fine," I told her, cutting her off a bit as she talked about something I wasn't even paying attention to. "What I want to know is, what's up with this roommate?"

She smiled. "Don't worry," she reassured me. "She'll be here soon."

I almost didn't hear her, because as I looked out the large wall of windows on the right side of the cafeteria, I saw a beautiful, dark-tanned blonde walking down the sidewalk. Now, the university was having back-to-school celebrations, so the cafeteria was jammed with people. But suddenly I could only see one of them. In my mind I said, "How cool would it be if that was Julie!"

I kept watch as this woman turned from the sidewalk toward the doors of the cafeteria. My intrigue was replaced by nerves, bordering on panic, as Joanna excitedly waved her over. As I realized I had been watching Julie walk up, I broke out into a cold sweat, and my palms got wet; a chill ran through my whole body, and I didn't know what to do.

Be cool, I told myself over and over as Joanna introduced us. "Greg, this is Julie. Julie, this is Greg." *Act natural.* I probably looked like someone who was making a big effort to act natural. But I did manage to speak in coherent sentences.

That's what I remember about meeting Julie. The beauty was the first thing I noticed. With her tan, she was darker than I was, and I'm African-American! And that blonde hair! I hadn't seen anyone like her before.

I remember she had this little feather earring in her left ear. And just as an excuse to touch her face, I reached out, as if I was interested in the earring, and toggled it a couple of times, letting my hand brush against the side of her face.

We started talking, and I think we both forgot about our friends. All around us there was the noise and chaos of hundreds of people in that big cafeteria, but the only thing I could think about was Julie.

*   *   *

I could see the walkway from the women's dorm to the cafeteria from my dorm room window, and I made good use of that view. I would sit there and watch for Julie and Joanna. When I saw them, I would rush out and then just *happen* to run into them as they were making their way to the cafeteria for lunch or dinner. (I didn't care too much about breakfast, because I hated getting up in the mornings.) I'm sure they eventually figured me out, because this happened too many times to be a coincidence.

One day I caught Julie between classes and asked if she was going to the back-to-school dance that weekend. She said that she'd be going with her friends, so I said maybe I'd see her there. Of course, there was no maybe about it. If she was going to be there, I'd make sure she saw me.

When my roommate and I got to the dance, I managed to find Julie and her friends. After some small talk I asked Julie if she wanted to dance. She said she didn't dance. I was surprised, but I brushed it off. After some more small talk, I went back to hang out with my roommate and some of the other guys on the basketball team.

I was still talking with them when the next song started, and when I looked down at the dance floor, I saw Julie out dancing with some other guy. *What's up with this?* I thought. Was she just trying to brush me off? I wasn't going to give up that easily. So I went over to the stairs and waited for her to come off the dance floor. Then I said to her, "I thought you said you didn't know how to dance."

She laughed. "If you can call that dancing, then I guess I can dance."

I smiled and invited her outside to talk, and she surprised me a little by accepting the invitation. We sat on a bench under a cluster of oak trees. It was a perfect night, with the stars shimmering against the background of the dark sky. After a few moments I got up the nerve to ask, "My roommate and I are going over to a party at a friend's apartment. Would you like to come with us?"

I made myself contain my excitement when she said yes. Sometimes it's hard to be cool and act natural at the same time, but I managed.

*   *   *

We made it to the other party, but I can't tell you a thing about it, because we never even went in. There was something different about this woman—I knew it. We sat outside the apartment complex by the pool from eight o'clock till two o'clock in the morning, and we did nothing but talk. I was opening up and revealing to her who I was, where I came from, girls I'd dated, my whole life story. And we were sharing our dreams, our hopes, our plans. I'd just met her, but I felt as though I knew her better than I knew anyone else.

As it got later and later, I was more and more sure that I didn't want to lose her. I wanted to do something or say something that would show her how I felt, and I desperately hoped that she was feeling the same way.

I had a gold heart that I wore on a chain. Just before we parted that night—or really that morning—I took it off and gave it to her.

"Look," I said, "whenever you feel like you don't want to be around me or talk to me anymore, you can give that back to me."

She took the heart and looked straight at me, and I waited, breathless, to hear what she would say. Would she laugh at me? Would she give the heart back?

She smiled at me. "I think I'm going to end up wearing it for the rest of my life, because I think you're the kind of guy that I want to marry."

That was August 31, 1984. The first night we went out still seems as if it was just yesterday.

I walked on air all the way back to my room.

* * *

I remember getting back to the room and telling my roommate, "I think I've found the girl I want to marry."

He laughed and said, "Get out of here."

Now, I have to tell you a little about myself. I always had girls who were interested in me back then. It's hard to say this without sounding like I'm bragging, but it's the way it was. I was on the basketball team, and there were always girls who went for me just because I was an athlete. And I didn't discourage a lot of them. So that's why my roommate kind of blew me off. I wasn't the type who just started talking about marriage the first time I met a girl. I usually could skip that because it wasn't even in the equation. But this time I said, "Man, I'm serious. e's something different about her."

And I meant it. Yes, she was beautiful, but I knew other beautiful girls. This really was different. For the first time I knew what it was like to be in love—not just lusting after a pretty girl but really thinking about spending the rest of my life with a woman. I felt as though something had been missing from my life until now, and now that I'd found it, I didn't want to lose it.

Julie felt the same way. I know, because she tried to deny it.

She was a freshman, away from home for the first time, and she'd been looking forward to having some fun at college. She didn't think that a serious relationship would be conducive to the sort of fun that she was looking to have at school, nor did she want to decide the course of the rest of her life at this present moment. After all, doesn't our culture tell us that we're supposed to play around in college? You know, have a lot of relationships, but not serious ones? It's supposed to be our time for parties and fun and maybe casual sex with people we barely know. Isn't that the way we see it on TV and in the movies?

So she thought, *Hey, I'm a freshman in college. I had no intention of coming to college and meeting someone serious.* And she was getting a lot of attention from other guys—something she'd never had in high school. So she broke up with me because she didn't want to deal with what she called the "pressures" of having a boyfriend.

"I'm just not ready to get serious," she told me. "I just got to college. This is my first time away from home, and I need some time."

I told her that I understood (though I really didn't want to understand). And I told her I'd be there if she needed me, I knew what she meant, and all I wanted was whatever would make her happy. But I really just wanted to kick something!

Still, I wasn't going to let that show. If she was going to have fun, I was going to have fun too. The next day I hung out with Lisa for most of the day, and I know Julie noticed. (To this day she doesn't care too much for the name Lisa.) That night I went to a party with my friends, and there were plenty of women paying attention to me. Then I noticed Julie with her friends, looking over at me from across the room.

Our breakup lasted for about a day. Julie found I was too irresistible and had to come back running. I'm not sure she'd tell the story that way, but I'm telling this part, so I get to tell it the way I want to tell it.

"I know I told you I wasn't ready to get serious with someone," she told me, "but it just tore at my heart when I saw you walking around the campus with other girls. So now I'm sure there's something special about you. I want to be with you."

*   *   *

After that we were pretty much inseparable. I suppose you could say we had your average college relationship: We went to parties together and did the sorts of things you do when you're in college. But we were a couple, and we were pretty sure it was meant to be that way. We did everything together—we ate together, we went out together, we spent whatever time we could together. As we went on through our college years, things progressively got more serious.

The one thing we didn't do together regularly was go to church. We didn't do it separately either.

The unfortunate truth is that, even though we went to a Catholic university and my dorm room was less than fifty yards from the chapel, we never thought much about going to Mass. I remember a couple of times when we did go, but I don't even remember what made us think of going then. It wasn't because we loved the Mass or because we wanted a closer relationship with Jesus Christ. The faith aspect of our lives just wasn't there. And that's probably why our relationship didn't go the way it should have gone.

I don't mean that we were miserable yet. We thought we were very happy together, and I suppose we were. But it wasn't an authentic happiness. It was the kind of happiness that comes from getting what you want right now, like eating candy. It wasn't the kind of happiness that leads you higher and higher toward heaven.

It's true that my relationship with Julie was very different from any other relationship I'd had. God was leading me to think the right thoughts, I'm sure of that. I was thinking of being with Julie for the rest of my life, and that was a big change for me. But I didn't really know *how* to think those thoughts. And that was why I had problems.

*   *   *

It isn't surprising that I didn't have much of a foundation for thinking the right way about my relationship with Julie. You have to understand something: I didn't really have any guidance. When I was growing up, my father never gave me the proverbial birds-and-bees talk, and I never had anyone I knew and trusted in the Church sit down and talk about chastity, sex, and sexuality. I was just left to pick it up on my own. So I did.

Ignorance about sex is a big vacuum that our human nature is going to fill as quickly a possible. If we don't teach our children about it ourselves, they're going to get it from somewhere. And popular culture is eagerly waiting to stuff their heads full of its own twisted version of the truth.

My source for that kind of knowledge—my catechesis, as I sometimes call it—was *Playboy* and *Penthouse*. As I grew into a teenager, those ideas became more and more a part of my life. I guess you could say it was not only my catechesis but a practical instruction manual too. It taught me how to *use* women very well. I learned how to use a woman physically, of course. But even when there wasn't a woman actually there, I knew how to use women *mentally*. I could conjure up the images I had seen and think, *Oh, wow, what I would do if I had her!*

This was confirmed by all of my friends. In the locker room sex was always the topic of conversation. I figured it to be just "normal" to view a woman this way.

"You have heard that it was said, 'You shall not commit adultery.' But I say to you that every one who looks at a woman lustfully has already committed adultery with her in his heart." That's what Jesus said about it (Matthew 5:27–28). It's what we *think* in our hearts that makes the sin.

So at a very early age, I began violating the dignity and worth of women.

Even so, I know that God was always working on me, trying to pull me in the right direction. God works with what we give him, and even my own backward notions of sexuality gave God something to work with, because they were at least part of what allowed me to know and understand that there was something different about Julie. Even though she possessed the physical attributes that I was attracted to, I didn't start out wanting to *use* her, the way I had done with other girls.

I remember that kind of striking me: I had a sincere desire to know *her* as a person, not as an object. That was different. There was something in my love for her that was very pure, even chaste.

* * *

Unfortunately it didn't stay that pure. It eventually led to the other part. I didn't know any other way of having a relationship with a woman. By October of that first year, we had a sexual relationship.

And I think that's the point in our relationship when we started losing the ability to really get to know each other. As soon as it started, the sexual relationship became paramount.

Before the sex there was always something to talk about. We talked about the future, about where we came from, about wanting to get married, and all these other things. But after sex entered the relationship, those kinds of conversations stopped. We just went to parties and came back and had sex. And at that point we robbed each other of the opportunity to continue to get to know each other as persons.

I think Julie feels the same way, but I'll let her tell you about that herself.

Before you go on...

Think about how your relationship with your spouse started.

• How did you first meet?

• Did you think right away that there was something special about this person? Or did that happen more gradually?

• What would you change about the early part of your relationship if you had it to do over again? Did you start habits then that have caused trouble for your relationship?

The Missing Ingredient

GREG TOLD YOU ABOUT HOW he grew up with no guidance from his father. I didn't have that excuse.

I grew up in what most people would think of as a perfect Catholic family. Certainly my parents didn't neglect teaching me about the Catholic faith. In fact, my father had gone to seminary for three years, so he knew what Catholic teachings were and how important they were.

The words I heard—"Don't have sex before marriage"—were just what you'd expect to hear in a family like that and just what I should have heard. But something strange happened as those words went from my ears to my brain. They got translated into this: As long as my parents don't know, I can do whatever I want.

To me religion was a set of rules about not doing what I wanted to do. For me the faith had nothing to do with God. I was sort of living my faith through my parents: I was Catholic because they were Catholic, not because I really had a personal relationship with God.

I saw a good example in my parents, but I thought that was for *them*, not for me. And that's not really their fault. You can only give your children what you know, and they did that.

I was lured away by the seduction of the culture. And the culture told me sex was just fun. You can have a rule, "Don't have sex till you marry." But then you have sex, and it feels so good, so how can this be bad? Why would people say not to do this? What's the big deal?

*   *   *

When Greg and I started school the next year, we actually got an apartment near campus and moved in together. By this time sex was the core of our relationship. We justified our living together with the fact that we were going to get married one day.

And that's where the troubles in our marriage began—long before we were married.

Look at the rise in the divorce rate, and then look at the rise in cohabitation. It's not just people who've been married three years who are getting divorced. It's people who've been married ten, twenty, thirty years.

When you base your relationship on sex, you're doing something against God and against each other. Then you carry that all through your relationship. You carry that into your marriage. And it really poisons everything. You may not realize it, but years later you're still carrying that thing with you.

I mean, I thought I had something really good with Greg. But if it was *good*, then why did I have to lie to my parents about it? What we failed to realize at that point was that we were also lying to each other. We were speaking a language with our bodies that only a married couple could speak. We were literally conditioning ourselves to sleep with someone without having to be in a committed marriage relationship.

Again, the foundation was weak, and it was not a foundation built on the rock. Jesus simply admonishes us,

> Every one then who hears these words of mine and does them
> will be like a wise man who built his house upon the rock; and
> the rain fell, and the floods came, and the winds blew and beat

upon that house, but it did not fall, because it had been founded on the rock. And everyone who hears these words of mine and does not do them will be like a foolish man who built his house upon sand, and the rain fell, and the floods came, and the winds blew and beat against that house, and it fell; and great was the fall of it. (Matthew 7:24–27)

And boy, did we experience the rain, floods, and wind! And our house indeed collapsed.

*　　*　　*

That fall my parents called and said, "Hey, we're going to come visit you guys for Thanksgiving."

Here we were living together in this one-bedroom apartment with a king-sized waterbed. What would my parents think? For me living together was all right, but I knew my parents couldn't find out about it.

So we came up with one of those schemes that never work in situation comedies. (And why did we think it would work better in real life? I don't know.) We decided to pretend that I had moved into the apartment on my own, and Greg was living in the dorms.

We planned to go out to dinner the day my parents came into town. So we picked them up at the airport and dropped them off at their hotel. Then we went to our apartment and got dressed. Then we hopped in the car, and I drove Greg back to the dorm and dropped him off there. Then I drove to the hotel and picked up my parents, and then we drove back to the dorm and picked up Greg, as though he'd been getting dressed there. (Can you hear the canned laugh track in the background yet?)

Perfect! Everything went off without a hitch. Or so I thought.

We went to an evening Mass, and then I sat in the back with Mom while Greg drove us to the restaurant. We stopped at a red light, and as we were sitting there, we started talking about what we were going to do after college. I said, "I think I'm coming home to plan for the wedding."

"Well, you know," Dad said, "I think that's a pretty good idea, because you need to get out of your current living situation."

He knew!

Poor Greg! He was just like a deer in the headlights. He was looking at me in the rearview mirror, and I was in the back seat next to Mom looking back at him, and we just knew that, that night, all the stuff was going to hit the fan.

Actually, Dad was far more composed than I thought he would be, although he was really disappointed in me. The living together was bad enough, but the one thing that pierced his heart was the fact that we had gone to Mass earlier that evening, and Greg and I had received the Eucharist.

"Living together is one thing," he said. "But what I can't understand is, how could you go up and receive Jesus in the Eucharist?"

What was the big deal? Everybody else gets up, files in line, and gets it, and so we did it too. I look back now with a feeling almost like horror, because I'm so much more aware of the power of the Eucharist. But then Greg and I had no concept of the real presence of Christ in the Eucharist.

*   *   *

I realize now that I did a lot of things because everybody else was doing them. I had sex with Greg because our culture told me that's what everybody does, and it's what women do if they want approval and to show their love. I moved in with him because, once again, that's what everyone was doing. If I was in church and everyone was standing up and getting in line, I did it too. I didn't have deep reasons for what I did. I wanted certain things, and I saw that everyone else was getting them, so I might as well get them too.

In a way, I suppose, it was a girl thing. I wanted people to like me, because our culture tells girls especially that's what's important. Maybe boys can be lone wolves and be cool, but girls are supposed to look for approval. In some ways I was more interested in having *somebody* like me than having Greg in particular like me.

Back in high school I had always felt as though my friends got more attention than I did. Some of them did things to get attention that they obviously shouldn't have done, but what I saw back then was the overtures they got, not the moral questions about how they got them. So now that I saw that I could have that attention too, I was doing whatever I could to be accepted. Maybe it meant going against my beliefs, but that attention was important to me; it felt good. I could set aside my beliefs if they were standing in the way.

I was selfish, wasn't I? But we're all selfish, and it takes a lot of work to overcome our selfishness.

*   *   *

When we finally did get married, I had the perfect wedding I'd always dreamed of, because every woman deserves to get the perfect wedding she's always dreamed of, doesn't she?

I must admit, it was almost a disaster. But that's one of those funny stories that make the memory of the wedding all the more perfect.

After college Greg had gone into the army. He'd gone back to Houston after graduation, anticipating a job with Technicolor at NASA. But that was just when the Challenger accident happened. Everything at NASA was put on hold, and the economy in Houston went into a tailspin. Greg had to make do with a job as an inspector at the Grocer's Supply Company warehouse.

I don't have to tell you that it wasn't anything like what he had hoped for. He'd been hoping for a professional career after college, not a job a high-school dropout could do. And that's where the army stepped in.

The army offered to train Greg, give him a job for four years, and set him up in a career as an X-ray technologist. It seemed like a great opportunity. He completed his basic training at Fort Bliss in El Paso and began his X-ray training at Fort Sam Houston in San Antonio. As he was nearing the completion of X-ray school, it was getting time to be assigned his permanent orders. This is typical, but the problem that it posed for us was that if Greg received orders to go overseas, I would not be able to accompany him, because we were not married. So that gave us the motivation we needed to get married as soon as we could.

Greg went to the chapel and looked around until he found the Catholic priest. It must have been a funny conversation. "Hi, Father. My name is Greg, and I'd like to get married."

Of course, the priest explained that in the Catholic Church, there was a little more to planning a wedding than just showing up and setting a date. But Greg told him that we'd already completed our pre-Cana course (although nothing in that particular course prepared us for what we were going to experience in our marriage).

"Well, in that case," the priest said, pulling his calendar out of his desk, "how soon did you want to do something?"

So we set a date only two weeks away, and I had two weeks to get my perfect wedding together. On that short notice we could invite only our families, a few mutual friends from college, and some of Greg's new army buddies. But that wouldn't stop me from making it a romantic little wedding.

We got married on a Friday evening. Greg wasn't able to pick me up at the airport, because he was scheduled to be in class until 5:00 PM. He'd asked his instructor if he could be dismissed early, because we still had to go pick up the marriage license at the courthouse, but his instructor said no. I don't know why not—it's just one of those things that happen in the military. But at ten minutes to five the instructor decided to let him go. So there we were, dashing from the Academy of Health Science to the car to get downtown to pick up our marriage license.

"We're never going to make it," I cried. "We're not even going to be able to get married today!" As if things weren't bad enough already, we started to get lost in downtown San Antonio.

But God knew what he was doing when he matched me with Greg. Greg calmly reassured me that everything would be OK, and that someday we would look back on this and laugh. Even then I appreciated his calm demeanor, because I certainly wasn't calm. And now I'm looking back and laughing—because of course, we did get our marriage license, and we scrambled back to base just in time for the wedding.

It was small and simple but beautiful. I had a beautiful dress, a good-looking groom, a nice chapel. Everything was picture-perfect.

Then came our wedding night, and—well, it was no big deal. We'd already been having sex for years, so what was some "I do" at the altar going to change about our being together?

But we were married, and now we had a problem. Popular culture tells us all sorts of stories about how people get married, but the stories usually end with the marriage. What's married *life* supposed to be like? Where are we supposed to go *after* the picture-perfect wedding?

As Greg will tell you, we really had no idea.

Before you go on...

Think about when you were engaged.

- Were you developing a good foundation for combining your two families? Or were you doing things you hoped your family wouldn't know about?
- Were you developing habits of openness and honesty or habits of sneaking around—either with your fiancé or behind your fiancé's back?

How Do You Do This "Marriage" Thing?

HERE'S A STORY I LIKE to tell.

A diocese had a new bishop. This bishop loved the faith like no other, and he wanted to know what the kids in the diocese were learning in regard to their faith. So he decided to visit the local Catholic high school the very next week.

The bishop went to a theology class. He introduced himself as the new bishop and told the students his reasons for being there. Of course, the kids all wanted to do their best to impress the new bishop.

He started out by saying, "So I can get some understanding of what you've been learning about the faith, I want to ask you a few questions. The first question is this: Who can give me the scriptural support for the sacrament of reconciliation?"

Immediately a girl in the front row raised her hand and said, "I know, Bishop! I know!"

He said, "Well, what is the answer?"

She said, "Bishop, you can find that in John 20, where Christ says to the apostles that whatever sins they forgive are forgiven, and whatever sins they retain are retained."

The bishop said, "Outstanding! Good job! All right, here's the second question. Who can give me scriptural support for the sacrament of the Eucharist?"

A guy raised his hand. "Bishop, you can find that in John 6, where Christ said to the apostles, 'If you eat my body and drink my blood, you remain in me, and I in you.'"

And again the bishop said, "Outstanding! You guys are sharp. I can tell right now I really don't have to be here. But one more question before I go. Who can give me the scriptural support for the sacrament of marriage?"

Well, all the kids in the room looked at each other with these blank stares on their faces. But then, very timidly, a guy in the middle of the room began to raise his hand.

The bishop acknowledged him and said, "Do you think you know?"

He said, "Well, I think so, Bishop."

"Well, go ahead. Give it a shot."

"Well, Bishop," he said, "I can't tell you exactly where it says this in Scripture, but I believe it's the part where it says, 'Forgive them, Father, for they do not know what they do.'"

That boy in the story actually knew a lot about what marriages are like today. Julie and I had been living together for a while, and we had no idea what it meant to be *married*.

*   *   *

But we were married now, whatever that meant, and I was in the army. We had our happy ending, except that we were just starting to realize that it was only the beginning.

The army is hard work, and one of those army experiences I'll always remember is going through the primary leadership development course. Part of it was the "Land Navigation" test. They dropped us out in a desert—for me it was the White Sands Missile Range—and gave us a canteen, a compass, and a map. The objective was to be able to figure out where you were and then find a series of points on the map from a list they gave you.

I knew going in that this wasn't going to be the most pleasant day of my life. It's really hot in the desert, and I only had so much water, and I had to do a lot of walking around. But I had to do it. The only way to get back to base was to go through the exercise.

Now, the first thing you have to do when you're beginning this process is to find out where "true north" is. It's called true north because there's only one north. There's not a "kind of" north, "maybe halfway" north, or a "sorta" north. There's just north. And if you don't orient yourself to the true north on the map, you'll find yourself completely lost. So you have to use the compass to help you find true north and turn your map to where north is. That's how you pinpoint your location.

You probably wonder why I'm making a big deal out of this little exercise. This is actually one of the stories I always tell married couples in our classes and talks. And when I'm telling this story in front of an audience, I like to have them do a little experiment.

"Stand up and close your eyes," I tell them. "Now slowly extend your finger, and turn to the direction you think is north. Then I tell them to open their eyes and see where everyone is pointing."

Of course I get a big laugh, because people are always pointing in all directions. If I had to depend on people's guesses about where north is to get me to Canada, I'd probably end up somewhere in Mexico.

In spite of what we may think, true north is only in one direction. And without knowing where "true north" is, you're going to get lost, I assure you.

It's just like that in our marriages. In spite of what we may think or feel about marriage, true north can be found in only one direction—up! *God* is true north for our marriages. God gives us what we need to know.

Quite simply, if our compass is not directed to what God is asking us to do in our marriage, then we're wrong, and *we* have to change. Not God, not the Bible, not the Church. We're the ones who are facing in the wrong direction. *We* have to change and live life—in this case, marriage—in accordance with how God has designed marriage.

Julie and I thought we knew what we were doing when we got married. But when I look back now, I realize we hadn't a clue as to where north was—or that there was a north in the first place.

*   *   *

My first assignment in the army was at Fort Bragg, North Carolina. I worked as an X-ray technologist at Womack Army Community Hospital. And the time we spent in North Carolina was the first time church became—well, I don't want to say it was important to us, but we did start going to church sometimes. Why? For the wrong reasons, as usual.

We had started having what I can only call a string of bad luck. We got the TV paid off, and then we had a big storm that fried the board on the TV. We were having car trouble, and repair bills were eating us up. All sorts of little things happened that cost us money and made us feel sorry for ourselves.

For some reason we thought about going to church. And then when we did go to church, life started to work out. Things were kind of OK. The bad luck seemed to stop. So we put those things together: Not going to church is bad luck; going to church is good luck.

Once in a radio interview, we were talking about this, and the interviewer said something like, "So it was more a superstitious kind of thing, right?"

And I suppose it was. It had nothing to do with our relationship with God. We didn't even understand what it meant to have a relationship with God. It didn't have anything to do with wanting to receive Jesus in

the Eucharist. It definitely didn't have anything to do with going and listening to the Liturgy of the Word. We just went because life was better
when we did. We were doing what seemed to bring us good luck.

*   *   *

After we'd been in North Carolina for a while, we had our first child,
Christopher. We had him baptized, and again it was because that's what
you do—not because we understood what the sacrament meant.

In fact, we were so clueless that we asked my brother to be the godfa-
ther. Now, my brother is a great guy, and we all love him. But although
at that point he was maybe confirmed, he certainly wasn't a practicing
Catholic, and in fact he still isn't today. How was he supposed to help us
raise Christopher in the Catholic faith?

But we didn't think of an answer to that question, because we didn't
even think of the question. We thought we had things pretty well figured out. Now I look back and see just how little we really knew.

We had been in North Carolina a little less than a year when I managed to get a transfer to Denver, to Fitzsimmons Army Medical Center.
This was home for Julie, and she was especially glad to be back with her
family. I don't need to tell you how happy her parents were to be so close
to their little grandson. We spent a lot of time with Julie's family, and
that was the first time I really had an opportunity to see how devout
Catholics lived.

Now, we were *sort of* Catholic when I was growing up. My parents
converted to the Catholic faith when I was in third grade. I distinctly
remember going to Mass for the first time and seeing the altar servers
and stained-glass windows and all those things. They were really
impressive to a little boy who was seeing them for the first time, and they
made me want to be an altar server.

So my brother and I became altar servers, and we would serve anytime
we got a chance. In the summer we would serve every wedding and
every funeral. So I had a good introduction to the external forms of the

33

Church—the ceremonies and the props, so to speak. Unfortunately, I never grasped what the Church was and what she taught.

That was partially due to the fact that the faith didn't really follow us home. It was something we did in church, but we left it there when we walked out the door. I do remember a time when my parents went to the Catholic bookstore to get rosaries, and we were going to start saying a family rosary. But somehow that didn't last. Church was really separate from our home life. The same mentality went with me to middle school, high school, and eventually to college.

But being around Julie's family—seeing the different sacramentals around the house, the pictures, and the crucifixes—that was kind of an awakening. All you had to do was look around to see that they were really living out their faith. They were very involved, as they still are, in Respect Life Ministry. To me they looked like pillars of the community. Everybody was always talking about Bob and Mary Dalton.

I saw things in their lives, especially in Julie's father's life, that made a huge impression on me. He was always talking about the faith and how we should be incorporating it in our lives—always doing what he could to spread the gospel. He was a great model of a good, solid Christian man. We spent a lot of time talking, and though I still didn't have a full understanding of my faith, I got the feeling that I wanted to be like my father-in-law one day.

I know part of that desire came from the external things: His genuine love of God and the Church drew people's respect. I liked the attention my father-in-law got and thought I'd like to have some of that for myself. I could see that he was happy, but at the time I never really attributed his happiness to understanding and living the faith.

* * *

While we were still living in Colorado, we had our second child, Lauren. When we went to Julie's postpartum appointment, the doctor invited both of us into his office. He'd been thinking about us, he said.

"You know, you have the perfect family now. You have your son, and now you have your daughter. One of you needs to get fixed."

Isn't that what we'd been taught to expect? Two children is the perfect number, and you certainly don't need to go beyond that. In fact, having more children is, according to the world's standard, kind of selfish and a little strange. But what got my attention was the word *fixed.*

I said, "Isn't that something you do with animals?"

He laughed a little. "Well, let me explain to you the human version." And then he went on to explain how Julie could get a tubal or I could get a vasectomy.

So we began to talk, and I said to Julie, "Well, you know, you went through all the pain with having the kids. The least I could do is get the vasectomy."

I look back on that now and shudder a bit, especially because I can see how very good I thought I was being. I'd be a good citizen and a good husband by preventing more children from coming into the world, and I'd take on the burden of the surgery so Julie didn't have to.

I don't need to tell you that I didn't really understand the Church's teaching on contraception. In fact, I'd never really heard of it at that point. I thought I was doing the right thing.

But we certainly weren't being selfless—neither of us. After all, when our youngest child graduated from high school, we'd still be in our early forties. We thought of all the things we could do as a relatively young couple with our kids out of the house and starting their own lives. What a shame; instead of enjoying the gifts that we had been given and being a family, we were already thinking of what our lives would be like after they were gone.

*   *   *

Our marriage relationship was pretty good for the first few years—no real problems or issues. We were fine as far as material comfort went. We were always planning for things we might want someday.

While I was in basic training, Julie became a flight attendant. And then to maintain the flight benefit, she started working in the company store for Continental Airlines. This afforded us the opportunity to travel to a lot of exotic places—Hawaii, Mexico, Jamaica.

After I'd been working as an X-ray technologist, I eventually became the noncommissioned officer in charge of what's called a special procedure suite, where we did angiographies and that kind of thing. I did the purchasing for the department, meeting with the sales reps for all the different products that we were using: catheters, contrast media, guide wires, and all sorts of things. That's when I started developing an interest in medical sales. I could see that people made a lot of money selling those things, and I thought it would be great to have some of that money for myself.

So I began talking to the reps about what I needed to do to get into that field. Julie had a friend from high school who lived in Austin, Texas, at the time. Her husband was working for a pharmaceutical company, and his counterpart with a sister company was being promoted and moving to California, and she personally wanted to help find her replacement. We went to Austin for a wedding, and he introduced me to her. We hit it off immediately.

Eventually, through a long interview process, I was offered a job with this pharmaceutical company. So after I got out of the army, we moved back to Austin. Now all of a sudden I had this job that paid me the kind of salary that allowed us to start buying the things that we had always dreamed of getting. We bought a house, two new cars, and a boat, which we kept at a marina on Lake Travis. We thought we had arrived.

Although we didn't connect the dots at the time, it was after the vasectomy—just when it looked as if we were getting everything we wanted—when things really started to go wrong in our marriage. As Julie will tell you, we thought the stuff we could buy would make our lives perfect. But at the same time, she didn't even want to be near me anymore.

Before you go on...

Remember the early years of your marriage.

• What did you expect marriage to be like? How was it different from what you expected?

• Did you look to God, Scripture, and the Church to tell you what marriage should be like? Or were social stereotypes and popular entertainment more influential?

CHAPTER 5

Making a Ton of Money

LET ME TAKE YOU BACK, as Greg did, and tell you a little more about where I came from.

As we mentioned before, I came from a very devout Catholic family. Going to Mass on Sunday wasn't optional for us when I was growing up. I mean, you *went*, no matter what, unless you were on your deathbed. In fact, it was so important that, if I wanted to spend Saturday night at a friend's house, it all depended on whether or not the family was Catholic and going to Mass on Sunday. I wasn't allowed to miss Mass.

But I didn't understand my faith. That rule about not missing Mass—to me it wasn't because I loved the Mass or because I wanted to meet Jesus Christ there. No, it was just a rule my parents gave me. It was a thing I did for them, not for me and not for God. So naturally, when I went away to college, I didn't go to Mass very often. In fact, for the most part I went only when I thought my parents would find out if I didn't go.

When we started going to Mass again after we were married, a lot of the motivation was the same—especially after we moved back to Denver, where I felt that my parents could keep an eye on us. Even after we moved to Austin, I remember waking up on Sunday mornings to the alarm and telling Greg, "Come on, we've got to get ready. Let's go to church. Hurry! Let's go to church!" And all this hurrying to get there was because I didn't want my dad and mom to find out I wasn't going. I didn't want to disappoint my parents. It was also in Austin that I began to encounter a whole different set of influences that would impact my life negatively.

*   *   *

We hung out with several couples we knew from our college days. We were the only ones who had kids. So all these people were hanging out, going places, having fun—and we had kids. They'd ask, and you could sort of hear the sneer, "Oh, Greg and Julie, can you come, or do you need to get a *babysitter?*"

And we had to answer, "Well, yeah, we have to get a babysitter, and we can't stay out as late as everybody else, because we have to be home in time for the babysitter." Once again our priorities were out of order. Our children were put on the back burner because we didn't want to miss out on something.

Many of the women in this group of couples were very career-minded. Not that there was anything wrong with that, but whenever we got together, they would be really excited about the promotions they were getting, the money they were making, the places they were traveling to. To them those things were what made life worthwhile.

And then they would come to me, and their whole demeanor would change. You could even see their faces changing. And they would say, "Aren't you bored staying home with your kids? Do you get anything out of that? Doesn't it drive you crazy?"

Well, after a while I started buying into what they were saying. I didn't have a strong conviction about why I was staying at home being a mother. *Yeah,* I thought, *you know what? I am kind of bored. I don't get to talk to any adults. I don't get paid any money. I don't get thanked for what I* do. *It's truly the most thankless job in the world.* I thought I had to go do something to show my importance.

I've always been really competitive, and now I told myself that I'd show these people who was important. *I'm going to prove to them,* I said to myself, *that not only can I get a job outside the home, but that I can make more money than any of them.* I was absolutely determined to show them that I could be *somebody.*

Of course, that implies that as a mother I was somehow nobody. That's how I thought of it then: I was *just* a mother, not *somebody.* (Now I know that one of the most important things a mother can do is stay at home and rear her kids.)

But where would I look for this perfect job?

*   *   *

As it turned out, I didn't have to look far. At this time Greg and I were working out at a really prestigious health club in Austin. It was where all the *important* people came to work out. Wouldn't you know, a friend who worked at the club told me about a corporate sales position that was opening. He thought they had it filled already, but he felt I should apply anyway.

When I applied for the position, I found out that they were planning to hire someone they had already identified from within the company. But I wasn't going to let that stop me. I was told no three times, but I kept going back, saying, "No, you don't understand. I'm the right person for this job. Please, can I prove it to you? Can I show you?"

And finally I got the job.

This position provided an opportunity to make plenty of money if you made a lot of sales. And within a month I was on top. Every time an announcement was made on the intercom, it was "Julie, you have a phone call on line two." We'd go to our sales meetings every day, and my name was usually at the top of the board. Number-one salesperson.

Look at how much money she's bringing in! All the attention was on me. I loved it, and it made me even more driven and competitive.

And then I started getting the paychecks, and oh, my gosh! The money was more than I'd ever thought I'd make in my life. Holy moly, this was an amazing place to be!

The job also allowed me the opportunity to be around a lot of rich, beautiful, vain people all day, every day. All they seemed to care about were their looks and their money. And because I hung around them, I started to do everything I could to fit in. Looks and money became my main goals too.

I would wake up at 4:30 in the morning to go work out for an hour and a half, go home, get the kids ready and take them to day care, then work right until 6:00 in the evening, so I could get them before day care closed. Then I'd go to McDonald's drive-through to get them dinner, because I didn't have time to fix dinner. We didn't have time for family meals, because I had to get back to the office. But they were happy, because they had Happy Meals, right?

I took the children back to work with me, where there was also a day-care center. I would go make more sales, maybe work out one more time, and finally get home at nine or nine-thirty and go right to bed, because I had to get up in the morning and do it all over again.

I can hardly believe it when I look back on it now, but that was how I arranged my priorities. Work first, my looks and my vanity second, kids third, and Greg—well, I hardly ever saw him. I was on this relentless pursuit of money, but more than that, I wanted approval and attention. This month I might be number one, but I didn't want to disappoint my boss next month.

I never called in sick. I was never late. I was spending all my energy and my time where I felt most appreciated. And I felt as though I really was *somebody*.

*   *   *

We were certainly accomplishing things by our friends' standards. Now we could keep up with the most materialistic people we knew. As Greg mentioned, we had the house, the cars, the boat, and the toys—all these different things that society, and our college friends, said we needed to be important.

We used to keep what we called a dream book of what kind of car we wanted, what kind of house we wanted, the kind of trips we wanted to take, the different appliances we wanted in the house. Little by little we started acquiring those things. And that began to consume our lives. We spent six years living this kind of lifestyle.

Ironically enough, it seemed that the more things we bought, the worse our marriage relationship got. We'd been married for about nine and a half years now, and we were locked in this relentless pursuit of happiness, which we believed depended on *things*. I knew I was happy, because I had all the *stuff* to prove I was happy, didn't I?

So why was Greg unhappy? I remember the night he called me into the bedroom and told me he was feeling miserable.

When I look back on it now, I know how much courage it took for Greg to be able to do that. But then I was just mad at him. *What's wrong with this guy? How could he be miserable? Look at the money we're bringing in. Come on!*

I suppose I wasn't very supportive. Here Greg finally had the guts to open up to me, and I was just thinking that money and success were the road to happiness. He had more time to himself while I stayed busy, so he recognized his aloneness, while I covered mine up with doing stuff. I just thought he was being lazy.

And that was when I started thinking, *Uh-oh! I've married the wrong person!*

Instead of sympathizing with Greg or trying to understand what was wrong, I just worked harder and harder, which drove us further and further apart. At last I was offered a job in San Antonio, which was an hour and a half commute south. I took the job because the money was even more than I was making at my current job.

Well, you can probably guess what happened. Going back and forth every day got to be a little taxing, so I decided to get a place in San Antonio and go home on Wednesdays and weekends to visit Greg and the kids. So I saw my family, on average, two days and three nights every week. The rest of the time, I had my real life—the life where I was accomplishing things and making money and being somebody important.

I see this with so many couples I talk to now. They don't know each other anymore, because they're just too busy. Both husband and wife are working outside the home, and when they're not working they're taking the kids to every kind of activity, or they're busy in clubs. Every moment of their day is scheduled, just as mine was, and they never find the time to fit each other into their schedules. They think they're fulfilled because they're doing "important" things. They hardly realize that they've defined marriage and family as *unimportant.*

And they don't even have time to ask the question or even know to ask the question, "What does God want?"

I was so sure that this was what life was all about that I didn't really care that Greg was miserable. I didn't realize that these material goals were poisoning our marriage relationship. I didn't even admit to myself that I was miserable.

Before you go on...

Think about your priorities.

- What do you work hardest for in your married life?
- Do you put your career before your spouse or your children?
- Do you look to material things to make you happy?
- Is what you're devoting your time to something that would be pleasing to God?

The Embarrassing Details

BEFORE I PICK UP WHERE Julie left off, I should probably give you a warning: We're getting into some really personal territory here. When we've told our story, we've sometimes been criticized: "You guys are too open. Those are some things that you should keep to yourselves." Some people don't even like the fact that we use the word divorce, as though not talking about it will keep the problem from ever happening.

On the other hand, we talk to hundreds of people—priests and laity alike—who thank us for being so open. They tell us that hearing our story—with all the ugly details—brings hope to other couples. After all, people come to us for help when they're desperate. When they see that we made it through stuff that was at least as bad as what they're going through and probably worse, they know it can be done. They know you can save a marriage that seems to be broken beyond repair.

We keep sharing our story, like the Gerasene man whom Jesus told, "'Return to your home, and declare how much God has done for you.' And he went away, proclaiming throughout the whole city how much Jesus had done for him" (Luke 8:39).

*   *   *

As I told you before, after my vasectomy seems to have been the time when we really started to notice a big change in our relationship—both in terms of communication and in terms of Julie's lack of desire to be intimate. And as I also told you earlier, I learned everything I knew about relationships from *Playboy* and *Penthouse* when I was a teenager.

That didn't stop in college, and it didn't stop when we got married. Pornography was very much a part of our relationship. It got to the point where those things had to be a part of our lives in order for me to be excited, if you will, about engaging in the marital embrace. I was always trying to coax Julie: "Hey, let's put on a tape."

I had that kind of pornographic outlook outside the bedroom too. If we were out for dinner or just walking in the mall, I was very vocal about physical attributes I saw in other females. Somehow I never thought that my casual remarks might be having a negative impact on Julie. *For me it was normal.*

And I never told her she looked good in the same way, even when she started working out every day. In fact, it was just the opposite. "I like *those* legs over there," I'd tell her. "Why don't your legs look like that? This working out isn't doing you much good, is it? You, Miss Fitness Queen, if you're spending all this time away from home, then how come you don't have a body like that? I like this behind over here—how come your behind looks like that if you're working out all the time?"

Obviously, some of that was just my resentment coming out: I was angry that she had time for working out but not for me. I was trying to give her a way to justify to me why she should be working out all the time, because *I* was not getting the benefit. Once again, it was all about what *I* got out of it.

Is it any wonder she was starting to hate being with me? Later Julie confided that there were times when I put my hand on her shoulder, and ould cringe inside, because she couldn't stand having me touch her.

We were not able to explain it then, but we know now this was because she felt like an object that was being used—not a woman, not a wife, not a mother, but a thing. My attitude, my behavior, the pornography—they all made her feel a sense of revulsion when she thought about having to engage in the marital embrace. When we did, it had nothing to do with the loving, generous gift of self that marital love is supposed to be. It was all about what I would get from the experience.

In our culture men and women use each other. Our culture says that men use women for sex, and women use men for love, or so they think. Only it's not authentic love; it's just the feeling of being wanted. What's missing is God, who is the source of all love. When God is not number one in the marriage, we tend to make each other a god, and when the other fails you—and they will—where do you turn?

Think of a triangle. Imagine you and your spouse are on the base of that triangle, at opposing points, and God's at the top. Now, if you're both striving for a relationship with God, you grow together. But if God's at the top and you're moving away from God, you're moving away from each other as well.

Instead of God, we were looking for other things to fill the void inside. But that void, that hole inside, can only be filled with God. When we're going away from the very source that is intended to fill it, then the hole just keeps getting bigger.

We worked on our prosperity and never put work into our relationship. Whenever we went out, it was to a party or with a group of couples or friends. Our time was never just *us* together. I'd even criticize Julie for that: "How come we never go out together?"

And when we did go out in these groups, I'd pay more attention to the other women than to Julie. They seemed to enjoy talking to me, and I made the most of that, with lots of touchy-feely hugging and things of that nature. Julie would see me giving time and attention to these other women, even physical attention, and that would make her mad. Needless to say, this created fuel for resentment. And that resentment grew into disgust.

Maybe Julie should have just smacked me. Or at least she might have told me how she was feeling. But that's where her background actually worked against her.

You see, Julie's parents have a great marriage, and one of the things everyone who knows them will tell you is that they never argue. You just never see them having a fight or even raising their voices. If you're married, I don't have to tell you how unusual that is. It's great—don't get me wrong—but it's not what most marriages are like, even when they're good marriages.

But because she grew up in this home where she never saw her parents argue or anything like that, Julie equated arguments with being on the road to divorce. She didn't want to think our marriage was in trouble, so she didn't want to start an argument. And that meant she never shared with me her true feelings. She was afraid that even expressing them would mean that she was not a good wife. She would never think of keeping me from doing anything that she thought I liked.

So I just went on thinking there was nothing wrong with what I was doing. And in a way, Julie thought that too. *This is just what marriage is like*—that's what we both thought. Men think about sex all the time— not love, but sex—and wives just put up with it.

We don't hold back on the embarrassing details when we tell people about this part of our lives, because we both think it's crucial that people hear this. So many men do what I did and don't think there's anything wrong. So many women think, *Well, that's just what men are like.* And many of those couples feel that they're not in love anymore, and they don't realize it's because these attitudes are forcing them apart.

Of course, nobody ever told us these attitudes were wrong. Pop culture tells us that sex is something men take and women reluctantly give. But living that way makes men miserable, makes women miserable, and tears marriages apart.

I bet there are women reading this right now and saying, "Wow, this is exactly what I am feeling." And I'll bet there are men saying, "Is she really feeling like that?" Over and over we've had couples tell us that this part of our story gave them real hope. "If the Alexanders got through it," they think, "we can definitely do it."

That's what's so cool, because fast-forward to where we are now, none of that's an issue. It's amazing how our marriage is today, after all that. How did we make it? That's where you see the grace. It's all because we're doing it God's way. With God you can heal anything.

But back then I didn't even know there was anything to heal. Now I can see it from Julie's point of view. I always had to have those tapes, and I was always pointing out those other girls. She must have been thinking, *What does he need me for?* She didn't feel loved; she just felt used. Yet she told herself that this was all just what guys do.

In our talks and workshops, Julie says, "A woman's greatest desire is to be loved by another. When a person who professes to love you for life makes you feel dirty, cheap, and as an object just to be used, there is nothing more devastating in the world." It is such a shame that we men make women feel that they are only good for one thing. I was guilty of that in our marriage.

Here we were in what should have been the happiest, most exciting time in our lives, and we were making each other miserable. How did Julie and I get to that point where we didn't want to be together anymore? We didn't even want to be in the same house.

*   *   *

As far as the outside world could see, we were still the perfect all-American family. We were engaged in the culture of keeping up with the

Joneses, competing, seeing who could get more—while at the same time slowly drifting further and further apart. Again, there was no arguing or yelling or anything like that, just more avoidance than anything. And that wasn't so hard, since Julie was gone from four o'clock in the morning until about nine or nine-thirty in the evening.

Then I got out of pharmaceutical sales and started working for the same health club Julie did, as an operations manager. Even though we were working in the same building, we only saw each other in passing. By that time avoiding each other had become a habit.

What should we do about it? At first we weren't sure there was anything to do anything about. It seemed as if we would go through these phases where one of us would begin to acknowledge that something was wrong, but the other wouldn't be ready. Julie would say, "I think there's something really wrong. We need to work on our relationship." But I wouldn't be in the mood. Then I'd get in the mood and say, "You're right. Let's work on something." And she'd say, "Well, I'm not really in the mood." We just kind of seesawed back and forth.

Meanwhile we began to dabble in the world of network marketing, once again looking for a way to accumulate more wealth. This made our lives even busier. We never had time to rest as we went from one meeting to another, trying to make our business a success.

We were never satisfied. Complacency in our lives was not even an option. Our desire was to make a ton of money and hang out and have fun; that was our definition of success. We just knew that this was the element that was missing, and it was going to make things all right. That's what we thought.

While our personal relationship was breaking down, we seemed to have a solid business relationship. That was where we put all our effort. When it came to business ideas and ways to make money, anything that would help us get ahead financially or socially—we were right there together, the dynamic duo, exploiting our chances.

This is really important for all of us to think about. In our society what looks like success may be complete and total failure. We thought our real jobs were the ones that brought in all the money that bought all the expensive stuff, while actually our real jobs were to be husband and wife to each other and parents to our kids.

As a husband I've learned that one of my primary duties is to minister to the needs of my wife. I can help bring in the money, but if I'm not taking care of her emotional needs, then she won't feel that she has any value or worth in the marriage. She may not even know why she's not happy, but she won't be happy.

The same is true for women. If a wife is not taking care of her husband's emotional needs, she's missing her primary duty as a wife.

Can you remember what it was like when you first met? You demonstrated that you cared about the other person by writing letters, buying gifts, going on dates, and so forth. Of course, you didn't call these "emotional needs," but you desperately wanted to be the one who fulfilled them. You weren't even thinking about it, and no one ever taught you about it. You were just doing what came naturally, because you loved the other person, and you wanted to show your love. So you put a lot of work into the relationship. That's what "being in love" is all about.

But then you got married, and well, you forgot all that stuff. Jobs, kids, and life took you away, and you started to take each other for granted.

We think that "being in love" is just some spark that happens. Actually, it's a lot of hard work. We shouldn't mind the hard work, because the rewards are so great. Marriage can only work when we work at it!

That isn't what we think though. *Hey, we met, the spark was there, and it should just be an eternal flame. If it goes out, maybe I met the wrong person. Maybe you just don't do it for me anymore.* We don't realize that the "spark" went out because we weren't putting the effort into it anymore.

* * *

So if I'm not doing the things that make my wife feel that sense of value and worth, then naturally she's going to gravitate to whatever it is that makes her feel it. Julie started to spend all her time at work and working out, because that was where she felt that she had value.

Why do you think so many women go to work when they have children? Why do so many women think that raising their family is not that important? Because they don't get the affirmation and appreciation from their husbands at home. And with our keeping-up-with-the-Joneses culture, it's so easy to convince ourselves that we *need* that extra income.

Julie told you about the couples we hung around with from college. It wasn't just their comments about Julie's staying at home that made her uncomfortable. They were making money and getting ahead, so we felt that we needed to do that too.

But those weren't the only Joneses we had to keep up with. We were working at this affluent health club with a bunch of multimillionaires running around, and we'd get invited to their homes and their parties, and we just *knew* that we had to get where they were. We had to have the things they had and make the money they made.

I remember thinking, *Gosh, if we could make this much money, then it would be OK.* We would even spend the weekend driving in some of the affluent neighborhoods, looking at houses. I'd say, "Man, if we could get one of those houses, our life would be set! Look at that car. Oh, my gosh, if we could get that car, that would be it!"

Poor Chris and Lauren; we would get a sitter for them at least two to three days a week. We thought that they would benefit later from the time that we were sacrificing now, because we'd be able to buy them anything that they wanted. For now we had to be at every party and every event so that we could hang out and rub elbows with the movers and shakers.

We were on a never-ending search for fulfillment, something to fill up that hole in our lives.

*   *   *

All this time we were teaching our kids their religious education, going through the motions in church ministries, but still our faith was not a part of what we lived. Faith and church were something we did for that hour on Sunday. But from Monday to Saturday we'd be Greg and Julie, the go-getters, living the way that we thought we should live.

Our going to Mass in Austin had nothing to do with God. Julie was sure that her dad had such a close relationship with God that if we did not go, God would somehow tell him! Then again, maybe that was part of God's grace. At least we were going to Mass. But as I know now, we weren't living a Christian life.

Professionally we were doing great; personally we could hardly stand to be around each other. All the things I had cherished about Julie in the beginning were twisted to become things that I really hated about her. This wonderful gift that God had intended her to be for me became a burden.

This is what happens when a marriage relationship is breaking down. The things you once couldn't wait to do with joy in your heart for the other start to become the things that irritate you and frustrate you. And then, like Adam and Eve, you point fingers.

God asks, "Greg, why don't you love Julie the way you should?"

And I answer, "Well, God, because *she* does this, *she* is like this...."

Just as with Adam, that's not really the answer God wants to hear. Just as he was with Adam, God is waiting for us to admit our own responsibility.

We were both looking at marriage exactly the wrong way, asking, "What is this marriage going to do for *me?* What is my spouse doing for *me* right now?" Those were the feelings I had been conditioned to have about marriage. "And if she's not doing it for me, then maybe she was the wrong person to marry in the first place." That was the conclusion I drew. It didn't occur to me that, if I was not getting anything out of our marriage, maybe it was because I was not putting anything into it.

My problem wasn't Julie; it was myself. I should have been asking, "What am *I* going to do for this marriage? What am *I* doing for Julie right now?"

*   *   *

Julie was becoming more and more successful. And the more successful she became, the more she dressed to get attention. Why didn't I get the message? If she wasn't getting attention from me, she was going to get it *somewhere*.

Once again I was completely missing the point. The problem wasn't Julie; the problem was me. I don't mean that Julie never did anything wrong. We were both guilty. What I mean is that, if you want a marriage to work, you have to take responsibility for your own actions.

We've worked with hundreds of couples who get to this stage in their marriage, where they don't want to talk to each other anymore. All they want to do is criticize and complain. If you want to make your marriage better, that's not the way to fix it, I assure you.

Think again of the story of Adam and Eve. It starts in Genesis 2:18, with God deciding that it wasn't good for the man he had just created to be alone. He needed a helper. In some translations you see the word *helpmate*.

God brought all the animals to Adam one by one, and he named each one of them. But none of them appeared to be a "helpmate"; not one of them was suitable to be Adam's companion.

At last God put Adam to sleep and made Eve from Adam's own rib. When he woke up, Adam recognized at once that here was someone who was like him—someone who could love and receive love in return.

Why weren't the animals suitable? Certainly the horse is useful. With a horse you can plow a field, or ride to the next town, or pull a wagon full of grain. Or what about the dog? Dogs can herd sheep, guard your treasure, or protect you from wild animals. Cats can keep rodents out of your grain supply. Cattle can give you meat and milk. Sheep can give you wool to protect you in the winter. All kinds of animals do all kinds of useful things.

But only another human being can meet your *emotional* needs and assist you in growing in holiness. Holiness, keep in mind, is not a state of piety or anything like that but simply growing closer to God. That's what being a helpmate is really about—helping the other grow closer to God so that we may one day merit eternal life in heaven.

Once I'm married, one of my primary duties is to minister to my spouse. If I am meeting her emotional needs, that gives our relationship its value and worth. But if I'm not meeting her emotional needs, then I'm not being a helpmate. And if I'm not making her feel that sense of value and worth, then naturally she's going to gravitate to whatever can make her feel that.

*   *   *

After a short stint in the health club business, I decided to work full time with a network-marketing company that I knew was going to get us to where we "needed" to be. Julie and I agreed that, until I could build my income up to where we could replace her income at the time—and she was making really good money—she would continue to work.

But then she took a vacation and decided that she was not going back to work. We didn't talk about it or anything. She didn't share anything with me. Just all of a sudden one day she said, "I'm not going back to work."

Now there was even more tension in the relationship, because we were spending as much as we made. In fact, we probably spent more than what we made, using credit cards and the like. Our outflow per month in terms of bills and other spending was at least six thousand dollars, with the cars and boats and everything else. All of a sudden I was thinking, *How are we going to pay these bills with you not working?*

So then we started dabbling in a couple of different home businesses, but those didn't work. And then a friend told us about an advertising job in San Antonio, where Julie could make this amazing amount of money. So she went down and interviewed and got the job.

Considering how much we needed the money—because we *had* to have the cars and the boat and the TV and everything, right?—we agreed that it would be OK if she stayed in San Antonio. I remember we had many friends who asked, "You guys think that's a good idea?" Even my mom had questions. But we needed the money. That was what we told ourselves.

By this time our kids were in about third or fourth grade. Julie had volunteered in church to teach our daughter's religious education class. But now she was leaving for San Antonio, so instead of making the church find another teacher, I agreed to substitute.

One day as I was preparing for the class, this little third-grade book actually started to teach me. There was one session in particular that talked about prayer. The question I was supposed to ask the kids was "Do you ever pray to God? If you do, what do you pray about?"

I remember thinking, *If I'm going to have to ask these kids about praying to God, then I'm going to have to pray to God.*

That was a big deal, even though it doesn't sound like much. For the first time there was kind of a flicker of a light in my mind, telling me that there should be more to my life than what I was doing.

*   *   *

Meanwhile Julie was spending almost all her time in San Antonio. I remember one evening, while watching TV, I got this strange feeling in my gut that she was having an affair. I don't know where it came from, but the feeling was real. Instead of confronting Julie with my thoughts, I began to engage in relationships that brought me closer to the near occasion of sin.

I had become friends with a woman in Austin, and I began to confide in her. I started telling her how miserable I was, and when I began to suspect that Julie was having an affair, I told her about that, too. And she was very sympathetic.

Of course, it started out as just a platonic friendship, but we could tell that—I don't even want to call it emotion—lust was growing. We could feel that desire to be intimate. And I remember trying to justify it in my mind, saying to myself, *I can't confirm that Julie's having an affair, and if I asked her she wouldn't tell me, but this way if she is, then she won't be the only one.* In fact, I remember saying those exact words to a friend of mine.

So it was around the time that Julie left for San Antonio, in October 1997, that I had an affair with this other woman. I thought that this would make me feel better about myself, but it actually turned out just the opposite. I was now doing something that I had said I would never do. I was cheating on my wife.

Before you go on...

Ask yourself what you're doing to keep up your marriage—not what your spouse is doing but what you are doing.

- Are you still as attentive to each other as you were when you first fell in love?
- Is there some little thing you could do right now that would make your spouse happier?
- Is God at the center of your marriage? If not, do you want him to be?

Rock Bottom

GREG AND I WORKED HARD to convince ourselves that there was nothing really wrong between us. What's really sad is that, until the affairs, I would have never thought that there was anything *that* wrong with our marriage. Sure, we were miserable, we were lonely. But I wouldn't have said that we were having *marriage problems.*

The facade we kept up was so perfect, I half-believed it. We even had couples come to us and say, "You guys have a perfect marriage. We hope our marriage can be like yours."

Every once in a while, someone might see through the facade a little bit. Christopher was having trouble in school—we found out later that he was dyslexic. And at one point Christopher's teacher—she had eyes—said, "Are there any problems in the home?"

How dare she insinuate there were problems in our home! Of course there weren't any problems in our home! Yes, Greg and I were both feeling miserable, but we didn't identify it as a *problem.*

We found out after the fact that our kids would go to the counselor's office almost every day. We had no idea. The school never called us. Our children were left with the burden of carrying our heavy cross while we were out chasing our own dreams.

We were so much into making money that even some of the other people in the network-marketing company worried about it. At one of the company seminars, which were mostly just pep rallies, someone criticized Greg for leaving our kids at home and spending so much time working on the business. But we justified it by bringing up the money. "By the time our daughter is ready to drive," we said, "she'll be driving a brand-new Corvette. Then do you think she'll be worried about the time we didn't spend with her when she was little?"

That was our answer: We'll buy our kids stuff to fill any void in their lives! All the time we didn't realize that we were making our kids miserable—as well as leading them down the same path that we were on.

How did we get so self-absorbed? It sounds as if we must have been awful people! But we really weren't much different from millions of other couples. Many try to carry too many burdens, and their lives become convoluted.

*   *   *

St. Benedict said that forgiveness frees two people: the one forgiven and the one forgiving. You're going to see later how important forgiveness is. It's the only way to get rid of the junk we carry around with us.

Maybe because I've done so much traveling since we started our apostolate, I think in terms of luggage. Each one of us carries around what I call an emotional suitcase. We fill it up with all the feelings we get from our relationships. If something happens that makes us feel happy, that goes into the suitcase. If something happens that makes us feel miserable, it goes in too.

If the suitcase is filled with good feelings, it's fun to carry around. It's like carrying around a big bag of gifts that you can't wait to share with people. But it seems as though the bad feelings gradually crowd out the good ones. Somehow bad feelings take up a lot more space in the suitcase. One harsh word at the wrong time, one forgotten anniversary or birthday, and it already seems as though the suitcase is weighted down with heavy burdens that nobody wants to carry anymore. Then we add the pressures we put on ourselves: careers that take up all our time, activities that separate us rather than bringing the family together—and before you know it, that suitcase is overflowing with heavy stuff.

We hate carrying all that around, and who can blame us? So we look for ways to escape our burdens. Sometimes we turn to drugs or alcohol. Sometimes we turn to shopping. Sometimes it's pornography or infidelity. Sometimes it's work—it certainly was for me. I spent more and more time at work, because that was where I felt fulfilled and appreciated.

Sometimes we even bury ourselves in church ministries, hoping that constant activity and doing good for others will keep us from thinking about the pain. We've seen that more than once. "He has to understand that I'm doing God's work," a wife will say. And that's true. But we have to be careful to insure that we are not immersing ourselves in ministry to avoid problems or issues at home.

When our marriage isn't working right, we can end up going round and round in a spiral of escapes. Each attempt at escaping the misery just leaves the spouse hurting more, ourselves hurting more, and the marriage in worse shape than ever. Then we look for even more and stronger ways to escape the misery.

Soon we're showing the signs of all that luggage we carry around. We don't sleep well. Our appetite is all out of kilter. We can't concentrate, and we don't have the energy to do much of anything. We get mad at little things, and our patience is diminished. Nothing seems to make us happy. Our family can't understand why we're so moody, and we can't understand why they can't understand. We might even end up with headaches, tight muscles, and other physical symptoms.

These things all come up because we just don't know how to deal with that big, heavy suitcase full of ugly emotions. But if we can learn to recognize these signs—if we can remember that they mean something is wrong with our life and our relationship—then we're on the right track. Once we see the problem, we can start to work on the root cause of it.

Seeing the problem, though, isn't as easy as it sounds. We have all sorts of defenses against seeing the problem. I thought I was being a good mother and wife by working all the time, even though it meant never seeing my family. After all, that's what you have to do, isn't it? If your children are going to have the nice things they deserve, you have to work for them, right?

And if I couldn't spend all that time with them, I could always sign them up for more activities, so that they'd be doing something constructive. *What a good mother I am! Look how many activities my children get to do!* But all those things added even more tension, and life was stressful enough.

The dual-income family seems to be the norm today. Family obligations, appointments, activities, getting dinner ready, and getting the laundry done seem to complicate things even more. Before you know it, getting to church on Sunday can become a real pressure.

Your spouse should be a refuge from all that stress. But what happens when you've poisoned your relationship, so that the spouse becomes another cause of stress instead of a refuge?

In my case—and in Greg's, too—we started looking for someone else to provide that refuge. That meant we started being open to attention from the opposite sex.

*   *   *

Before Greg and I got ourselves in trouble, it was hard for me to understand how married people could have affairs. I remember hearing about other people's affairs and thinking, *Oh, my gosh; they had an affair? How could they do that?*

But it's not hard to see what happened with us. We set it up perfectly for each other, because we had stopped communicating a long time before. Then we began to communicate with other members of the opposite sex. "Your husband doesn't pay attention to you? Gosh, if I was your husband..." Men began to say things that I really wanted to hear from Greg. And he began to hear certain things from other women that he really wanted to hear from me.

I remember the first time it happened with me. It wasn't much: just a man at the health club saying, "You have nice legs."

Oh, my gosh! That's where my attention went, because I could never hear that from my husband. Not that I even thought of that, but I can remember my ears going *pop!* It was exactly what I was craving. It opened up the idea that maybe what I wasn't getting from my marriage was available outside of the marriage.

I was looking for some way to get rid of the junk that had accumulated in my emotional luggage, and here was a way. Just one little remark, and I felt better about myself.

Of course, I was looking in the wrong direction. But I didn't think about that. All I thought about was how much better I felt. This also ignited the doubt in my mind about my husband's love for me. If he really loved me, then I would hear these things from him—right?

Satan hasn't changed his tactics. This is how he tempted Eve in the garden. "Did God really tell you not to eat from any of the trees in the garden?" he asked. He tries to get you to doubt the love of the one who loves you the most. *Does Greg really love you?*

*   *   *

So if that was the wrong direction, what's the right direction? Scripture tells us what we should really be doing with all our burdens.

> Cast all your anxieties on him, for he cares about you. Be
> sober, be watchful. Your adversary the devil prowls around like

a roaring lion, seeking some one to devour. Resist him, firm in your faith, knowing that the same experience of suffering is required of your brotherhood throughout the world. And after you have suffered a little while, the God of all grace, who has called you to his eternal glory in Christ, will himself restore, establish, and strengthen you. To him be the dominion for ever and ever. Amen. (1 Peter 5:7–11)

When we're feeling worried or miserable, St. Peter tells us, we should let God carry our burdens. And then Peter immediately gives us a warning. Our enemy is prowling around, looking for his opportunity. Satan wants to weaken us so he can eat us up. We have a choice: We can leave everything in God's hands, or we can leave ourselves open to Satan's attack.

That's why it's so important to get God involved. Only God can really carry all those heavy burdens we want to get rid of.

We also have to be aware of Satan all the time. That means we have to see all the temptations around us for what they really are. They don't take our burdens away. They make us feel better for a little while, but then they pile even heavier burdens into our suitcase.

We're not alone in this. Every Christian has to suffer in some way. Even Christ had heavy burdens to carry. He sweated blood at Gethsemane, knowing what he would have to suffer. If we embrace our suffering the way Christ did, we can unite our suffering to his—and that can bring redemption to our empty lives and miserable relationships.

That's why St. Peter tells us to look to "the God of all grace," not to alcohol, or drugs, or pornography, or affairs. And I know he's right. St. Peter's way—God's way—is the only one that works!

But of course, Greg and I didn't find the right way until we'd tried the wrong way. And that's how we ended up in that devastating spiral of lelity and guilt, until finally we hit rock bottom. Our marriage was miserable. I wanted out. And that's when, by the grace of God, we got acquainted with the tribunal vicar in our diocese. Finally a way out!

Before you go on...

Think about where your spouse gets the most attention.

• Is it at home, from you? Or is it at work? Or is it at church?

• Are you doing what you need to do to make your spouse feel appreciated?

Dying to Self

WHEN JULIE TOLD ME SHE'D set up an appointment with the visiting priest, I thought, *Here we have this new friend, and you want to go and spill all of our junk. I'm not going.*

But we went. And we spent forty-five minutes saying, "He did this," and "She did this," and "We can't stand each other."

"Father, we're here to have you help us get out of our marriage," we said. "We need to get a divorce."

And he sat and listened the whole time—so graciously. Only when we'd said everything we had to say did he hit us with these questions:

What is God's plan for marriage?
What does our Church teach?
What do St. Paul and the Holy Fathers say about marriage?

This was exactly what we needed to hear, although we had never expected to hear it. We wanted to find out how to get out of our marriage, not to discuss marriage in general.

Later, when Father left the diocese to teach canon law at a university, he told us, "You know, that day you came in to see me, it was the Holy Spirit at work."

And I said, "Really, Father? Why do you say that?"

And he said, "With the nature of my work with the tribunal, I make it a point not to become friends with couples, because I never know whose paperwork is going to come across my desk for an annulment. So it was the Holy Spirit that made me say yes to have you guys come see me that day."

I believe him, because our visit with him was the beginning of many beautiful things that started to happen in our marriage.

*   *   *

If Father had sat there that day and preached at us, giving us the answers to those questions, would we have listened to him at all? I doubt it. But there was something about that challenge. He didn't just ask us the questions; he *challenged* us to go out and find the answers.

It worked so well for us that we still do that with couples today. And although you're going to find some of the answers in this book, I still urge you to go out and find them for yourself. Don't just take our word for it. Find your Bible—do you even know where it is? I didn't. In fact, when I found mine, I could write my name in the dust on the cover.

Read for yourself what Scripture has to say. Do the same with the *Catechism of the Catholic Church*. (The United State Catholic Conference of Bishops website, www.usccb.org, has an online *Catechism* and order information for paper copies.) Get those answers from the source.

In our marriage coaching sessions, we give couples an understanding about what God's plan for marriage is, but then their homework is to go back and look in the *Catechism of the Catholic Church*. Go to paragraph 1602, we tell them, and start with "Marriage in God's Plan."

I encourage you to do the same. Don't forget to say a quick prayer to the Holy Spirit, asking him to reveal to you what God wants you to know from this text. Understand this: God wants you to seek him out. You have to take ownership, so to speak, of your search. No one can do it for you. You can get help from your priest, from us, from other couples, but the search has to be your own. You have to want God to be part of your life.

*   *   *

When I opened our Bible, I started with St. Paul's letter to the Ephesians, because I remembered the homily we would hear every year about marriage. So I thought, *Let's see what St. Paul has to say about marriage.* And I found the words I remembered in chapter 5, starting with verse 22, "Wives, be subject to your husbands."

My immediate thought was, *This is what's wrong with our marriage! Julie just doesn't do the things I ask her to do. I've got a wife who's out wanting to make a million dollars and doing her own thing, and she's simply not doing the things that I want her to do in this marriage relationship.*

I was really liking this Scripture stuff.

So I went on. And in the next few lines I read, "Husbands, love your wives, as Christ loved the church" (Ephesians 5:25).

I remember thinking to myself, *How did Christ love the church?* And the answer was right there: He "gave himself up for her."

Christ died for the Church! I had to ask myself, *Am I dying to myself for some of the things Julie wants in this marriage?* And of course the answer was no. For the first time I really began to think that maybe—just maybe—some of my own selfishness was contributing to the breakup of our marriage.

*   *   *

There was a lot more to read—more in the Bible and then in the *Catechism of the Catholic Church.* As I read, it started to dawn on me that maybe I had some sort of responsibility to share this information with Julie. I don't even know where that thought came from, because at that point I had never heard anything about a man being the spiritual leader or anything like that. But if Christ died to bring the Word to us, I must have some sort of responsibility to bring the Word to my own wife.

So I went from the Bible to the *Catechism*. The section on marriage is incredibly rich. I started in 1602, where it talks about God's plan for marriage. By the time you get to paragraph 1606, it's talking about what happens in a marriage relationship once the regime of sin enters into it. And while I was reading about all the things that happen— "discord, a spirit of domination, infidelity, jealousy and conflicts that can escalate into hatred and separation"—I was thinking, *Wow! These are all the things we're going through! Maybe this Church does know something about marriage.*

And then a little further on, it tells us that in order to heal the wounds of sin, man and woman need the help of the grace that God in his infinite mercy never refuses them. "Without his help man and woman cannot achieve the union of their lives for which God created them 'in the beginning'" (*CCC*, #1608).

Bells started ringing in my head. *We're not even coming close! God is not the center in our lives. We go to church, but God is nowhere near the center.*

I was really getting into this stuff. I honestly think the Holy Spirit was leading me. So then I got on the Internet. Where would I look? (This was back in the old days, before Google; AltaVista was the big search engine back then.) So I just typed in "marriage catholic church," and that led me straight to the Catholic Information Network and Blessed Pope John Paul II's *Familiaris Consortio*, his apostolic exhortation on the role of the Christian family.

I started reading that document, just to get an overview. When I saw some of the things that our late Holy Father was talking about— the qualities and characteristics of the good Christian husband, the dynamics that should be part of the good Christian family—I knew I'd struck gold.

For two days I didn't go to work or anything—I just stayed in our bedroom staring at the computer and reading. Normally that would be a sign of serious depression, but I was really getting my life sorted out for the first time!

The second evening I called Julie into the room and said, "Julie, I want to share with you what our Church has to teach about the sacrament of marriage. No wonder we're screwing it up! We're not even coming close to living it—dying to self, God having to be part of your marriage in order for it to be a good marriage, and all these different things."

Well, when I shared all this with Julie, she was just as much in awe as I was. "This is incredible!" she said. "What are we going to do?"

And I said, "I think we need to pray."

Now, in our ten years of marriage, thirteen years of being together, we had never even thought of praying together, outside of the meal prayer and the Our Father at church. But now we got down on our knees holding hands, and I spontaneously went into prayer.

I said, "Father, we tried living our marriage based on the things *we* think we need to do, and it doesn't work. And we've also tried living our marriage based on things we've gotten from society, and *that* doesn't work. Heavenly Father, more than anything in the world, right now we sincerely invite you into our lives to show us how *you* want us to live this thing called marriage. And if you deliver us from this evil, we will commit the rest of our lives to working with some kind of marriage or family ministry."

I can't even tell you where those words came from. I just know that's what came out of my mouth.

* * *

Looking for information on God's plan for marriage eventually led us both to studying other aspects of our faith. It's hard to describe how exciting it was. "Oh, I didn't know this!" "Oh, wow, look at that!" We were both eager to share what we'd learned.

We started studying the sacrament of reconciliation. Up to that point everything that we had been taught about that sacrament, from what I can remember, dealt with going to receive absolution for your mortal sins. If you were feeling kind of bogged down, as if you had the monkey on your back, you went to the sacrament of reconciliation, and it would make you feel better. Those things are true, and they're good, but they should not be the reasons we go to confession.

Whenever I would read or study I would say a quick prayer to God, asking him to send me the Holy Spirit to reveal to me what He wanted me to know. Well, on this particular day, I felt the Holy Spirit saying that the reason we go to the sacrament of reconciliation is to reconcile with our Father. That hit me like a ton of bricks, and after all these years this finally made sense to me. Because once we engage in mortal sin, we sever our relationship with God, and the only thing that can restore that relationship is the sacrament of reconciliation. But first I had to go to the *Catechism* to find out what constitutes a mortal sin (see *CCC,* #1854–1864).

The Church teaches that when we're baptized, we receive sanctifying grace, and that washes away original sin. It's that sanctifying grace that allows us to reside in this wonderful relationship with God and to merit eternal life in heaven. But mortal sin and sanctifying grace cannot coexist in the soul. So if we commit a mortal sin, sanctifying grace is gone. Then we don't have that sanctifying grace to save us, and then we're on our own. So we can't do the things we know are right and can't make things work.

This was one of our most important discoveries. If God is at the center of our relationship, then our relationship with God has to be good before our relationship with each other can be good. That means we have to get those mortal sins taken care of.

When couples come to us, we ask, "When was the last time you went to confession?"

Some say two years, some three years, some ten years or more.

"Well," we tell them, "you should consider yourselves blessed for making it this far."

You have to understand that everything that we have, everything that we are, everything that we do—it all hinges on God's grace. My writing this sentence right now is God's grace at work. Your taking your very next breath is God's grace at work. Why? Because he wills it to be so. If he were to choose for you to cease to exist, he removes his grace and at that very moment you *would* cease to exist. Everything you have is a result of God's grace. We need to be mindful of it first of all, and then we need to be thankful.

*   *   *

We had always put material success at the center of our lives. Now we realized we had to put God there instead. This was a life-changing discovery for us.

How life-changing was it? About a week later we decided to quit our jobs. We were both working for the same advertising company, and we had the same boss. We typed up our respective resignation letters and handed them in.

Our boss said, "You guys, is this a joke?"

I said, "No, we're serious."

He said, "Well, what are you going to do?"

I said, "I have no idea."

"Now, wait a minute," he said. "You're *resigning* from this job? I know the kind of money you're making, and you don't have anything lined up. You guys are nuts."

I said, "No, John, we *used* to be nuts. Right now I think we're gaining a little bit of sanity about ourselves."

We walked out of the building holding hands. And as we cleared the building, I said, "OK, Father, we're yours. What do you want to do with us?"

Before you go on...

Read what St. Paul has to say about marriage in Ephesians:

> Be subject to one another out of reverence for Christ. Wives, be subject to your husbands, as to the Lord. For the husband is the head of the wife as Christ is the head of the church, his body, and is himself its Savior. As the church is subject to Christ, so let wives also be subject in everything to their husbands. Husbands, love your wives, as Christ loved the church and gave himself up for her, that he might sanctify her, having cleansed her by the washing of water with the word, that he might present the church to himself in splendor, without spot or wrinkle or any such thing, that she might be holy and without blemish. Even so husbands should love their wives as their own bodies. He who loves his wife loves himself. For no man ever hates his own flesh, but nourishes and cherishes it, as Christ does the church, because we are members of his body. "For this reason a man shall leave his father and mother and be joined to his wife, and the two shall become one flesh." This mystery is a profound one, and I am saying that it refers to Christ and the church; however, let each one of you love his wife as himself, and let the wife see that she respects her husband. (Ephesians 5:21–33)

Husbands:
• Do you die to yourself for the sake of your beloved?
• Are you the spiritual leader of your home? If not, why not?
• Does your wife allow you to lead her and your family spiritually?
Wives:
• Do you respect your husband?
• If not, what are some ways you can show him respect?

Learning to Forgive

WHAT *DID* GOD WANT TO do with us? I didn't know any more than Greg did. But I did know that I was going to follow him, and we were going to do something worthwhile.

That day he called me into the bedroom and started teaching me about the Church's teachings on marriage, it was as if I was falling in love all over again, but this time it was a totally different feeling. When he started showing me things, talking to me, reading to me from the *Catechism*—my heart, again, was on fire. This was the first time I really felt what *true love* was all about.

When we meet with a couple, I'll tell this story of how I felt when Greg started to lead me to Christ, and the women will always say, "That's it! This is what I want; I want him to lead!"

And many times the husband responds, "She won't let me!"

Really, the problem is that men have never been taught how to lead. Typically the father figures in their lives have never given a true example to their sons. It's the *moms* who are making sure they say the rosary and go to church; moms are making sure that the spiritual part is there. I think that when the men aren't doing it, the women take over and try to take care of everything, not allowing the men to really be the spiritual leaders. I believe that the deepest desire for a woman is to have her husband lead her spiritually.

When we take the couples through our marriage coaching sessions, we ask them, "What is God's plan for marriage?" They need to learn what Greg was teaching me—the stuff he had begun to learn with only two days of reading. They need to find out that God planned very specific things for marriage, and if we are not living them in our marriage, then we are not living marriage the way that God desires.

I remember the first thing Greg told me was "He gave us each other to learn to love as he loves." And that was so foreign to me, because the way we "loved each other" was not loving. It was abusing the gift we had been given and, to some extent, using. We were taking what we could get from the other and stripping each other of dignity and worth.

When Greg started teaching me what God planned for marriage, my feelings changed—right at that moment. I was open. I wanted to know more. I wanted to spend more time with Greg. I wanted to know what he was going to say. I was in love! And I still want to know more and to love him more to this very day.

*   *   *

From that moment on we knew everything had to change, and I do mean everything. We needed a total reconstruction of our marriage, from the way we'd come together at the very beginning to the present. We had to start all over, totally revamping the ways that we treated each other, our children, and anyone with whom we came in contact.

Reading and learning what the Church taught allowed us to reflect on how we were living. What were our priorities? I can remember making the list in my head: money was first; job was second (because that allowed me to make the money, and I had to have that); the kids were third; family and friends and stuff like that were next; and each other— we were last on the list. No, not quite last, because God was at the very bottom. When we were in trouble or didn't have the things we wanted, we went to God in prayer.

We realized that our priorities were totally upside down. And so we quit our jobs. The constant go-getting was one of the things that kept us stuck in our rut. In fact, we had to get away from anything that was not positively contributing to our marriage—things we did, places we went, even people we hung out with.

As my personal prayer life was starting to get stronger, I was soon led into a relationship with the Blessed Mother. I began asking her to show me what it truly means to be a woman. I thought, *What better person to show me how to do this than the woman God chose to bring his only Son into the world?*

I realized that I had been living in a way that was totally opposite of what I was created for. I was making a name for myself and, at the same time, losing myself to the world.

As my relationship with Mary grew, I was able to understand my own worth and dignity. I had this deep desire to please God more than anything in the world. Instead of praying that Greg would change into the man that I desired *him* to be, I finally prayed, "Help *me* to become the woman that you created me to be." As I became that woman, God gave me more than I prayed for, because I received a man who gave me more than I could ever dream of.

*   *   *

That doesn't mean everything was fixed right away. Forgiveness is hard work; don't think we're minimizing how much work it is. If you are open to the grace, the forgiveness can happen instantaneously, but it is the forgetting that may take some time.

At the same time, *unforgiveness* is a lot harder in the long run. St. Paul knew what he was talking about when he said, "Don't let the sun go down on your anger" (Ephesians 4:26). Unforgiveness poisons all our relationships. And the more a relationship is poisoned, the harder it is to forgive. You have to break the cycle somewhere.

One of the things we do when we work with couples is take them through a forgiveness and healing exercise, and it starts with an examination of conscience. If you're familiar with this practice, you probably already have an idea of what an examination of conscience is. We tell each spouse to take some time alone and really look at what he or she has been doing. "What did you say to your spouse that really stung? How did what you did, and what you didn't do, hurt your spouse and your relationship?"

This is really hard to do—much harder than it sounds. We have been conditioned to always point out the faults of others, and it's a lot harder to reflect on the things that we may have done to hurt our marriage. I could think of a long list of things Greg had done wrong, but it was hard for me to think of anything I'd done wrong. On the other hand, Greg could easily fill me in on what I'd done wrong, but he was having trouble remembering anything he'd done wrong.

That's what it's like being human. We see splinters in other people's eyes and miss the logs in our own (see Matthew 7 and Luke 6).

It's hard because we *feel* how much we've been hurt. But we never *feel* how much we hurt others. And the hurts aren't always the same kind or always equal.

Once a couple came to us, and the husband had been having an affair. Naturally the wife (I'll call her Mary) was very upset. She hadn't cheated at all; only her husband had.

So I asked her as gently as I could, "Mary, have you come to understand what you've done to contribute to your husband's infidelity?"

She was flabbergasted. She hadn't done anything wrong! Was I trying to excuse her husband's infidelity by saying she drove him to it? "I'm the victim here!" she practically shouted.

"I understand that," I said, and I meant it. "But have you come to understand what *you've* done to cause your husband to seek pleasure from someone outside of your marriage relationship?"

Of course, I was in no way trying to justify the husband's unfaithfulness. He had made a choice, and it was a bad one. That was his fault.

But if your relationship is breaking down and you think you haven't done anything wrong at all, then you're just not thinking hard enough. It takes two people to get to where you are in your relationship. Very seldom does a spouse purposefully intend to have an affair. There have been a few who believe it is their right because they are not getting what they *deserve* from their spouse—but there is nothing right about that.

Our culture tells us all the time that we *should* get mad. We *must* get even. People must pay for what they have done wrong. We watch TV shows in which people shout at each other for an hour, and we think that's the way we should face our problems. If our spouse has cheated on us, we're told, we *ought* to be mad. Maybe we should never forgive.

But as Christians we're held to a higher standard than that of daytime TV. We know that we have a choice about how we respond when others hurt us. Jesus told us to turn the other cheek. That's actually a freedom, because it allows us to release the anger that we usually hold onto. In the face of the world saying we have to get mad, our free Christian will can reply, "No, I don't have to get mad. I can *control* how I respond." We need to exercise that freedom if we want to save our marriage.

The story of Mary and her husband has a happy ending, by the way. I prayed a lot for her over the next week, and the next time we saw the couple, she told me, "I understand now."

She'd come to accept her part of the responsibility. She confessed the ways she would disrespect her husband in front of their children and other people. She admitted, "I am always too busy when he wants to do something with me or just sit and relax on the couch. I get tired from being busy all day with the children and am too tired to do anything with him." Admitting that responsibility was a vital step in putting her marriage back together.

Making an admission like that is hard. We're afraid to look at ourselves, because our pride might be hurt. We don't dare bring up old insecurities.

So one of the first things you have to do is rely on God. Remember that he has enough strength to hold you up even when your pride takes a tumble. To get through your first real examination of conscience, you need to ask for strength.

A good examination of conscience requires the freedom to think objectively about the past. We need to ask the Holy Spirit to show us what we've done wrong—and then open our eyes so he can show us.

And you can't just go back to the most recent argument and leave things there. Greg and I realized that a lot of the problems in our relationship went right back to the beginning. It's going to be the same with you. Think of what things were like when you were dating. Did you live together before you were married? Did one of you push the other into premarital sex? Even if there was no pushing, did each of you use the other, for sex or for status or anything else, rather than giving yourself wholly to the other's welfare? Events such as these can and will have a negative impact on your marriage, and you must put them to rest before they start to unravel the fiber in your marriage relationship.

Although you need to own up to the past hurts that you inflicted upon each other, you must be diligent about not allowing them to impact your future. Part of the forgiveness process is being able to forget. If you continue to struggle with a particular incident, just take it to prayer and ask God to give you the grace to forgive as he forgives. Remember, you are not in this alone: "I can do all things in him who strengthens me" (Philippians 4:13).

We came to recognize that, in our own relationship, we had started on the wrong foot. We began our relationship with a lie, because we were acting as though we were married when really we were not. Living together before marriage is a lie that causes a lot of issues with couples today. We justify it by saying that everyone else is doing it, and yet it is against God's plan. Thus we lie to ourselves, to one another, and to God.

What you didn't do all throughout the relationship is just as important as what you did do. If you've been to Mass lately, you'll remember the words of the Penitential Rite: "I confess to Almighty God, and to you, my brothers and sisters, that I have sinned through my own fault, in my thoughts and in my words, in what I have done and in what I have failed to do...." What you thought and what you said, what you did and what you didn't do—all can be damaging, and everything that was damaging needs forgiveness.

✢   ✳   ✳

After a couple have done this separate examination of conscience, we have them sit down together. First the husband will go through his whole list and ask forgiveness for everything on it. When the husband has done that, it's vital for the wife to actually say, "I forgive you." You can't imagine, until you've felt it, what a healing freedom there is in those words. You know you're forgiven, and your sins are behind you.

Then the husband asks if there's anything he left off the list. If so, he asks forgiveness for that too. The wife then goes through her list and asks forgiveness, and the husband responds.

The next part of the forgiveness and healing process is sincere contrition.

If you're up on your sacraments, you know that we call confession the sacrament of reconciliation. When we sin, we damage our relationship with God. That's the most important relationship in our lives. Damage to that relationship is damage to ourselves. Therefore we need to have sincere contrition for the sins that damaged it.

The same is true in our marriage relationship. Since the two of us become one flesh in marriage, we don't just hurt our spouse when we sin against him or her. We also hurt ourselves. If I've hurt my husband, I need to seek forgiveness and reconciliation; he needs to know that I understand how much I hurt him. That's what motivates me to ask Greg for forgiveness when I discover that I've wronged him.

*   *   *

The final part of the healing and forgiveness process is penance. We ask couples to go to the sacrament of reconciliation individually as their penance for the way they've hurt each other. There couples receive sacramental grace from God to complete the healing and forgiveness process.

We've both said it before, but we can't say it enough: Confession is *vital* to our lives and our marriages.

We've had couples tell us when we began coaching them, "I can't live with this person anymore," or, "I can't stand this person anymore." Our first question is, "When was the last time you went to reconciliation?"

"What does that have to do with anything?" they usually ask.

Once they finally tell us, the answer is almost always *years*— sometimes ten, twenty, or thirty years.

It's sad to see how many people don't make use of God's gifts! That's what the sacraments are—gifts, not rules to make our lives miserable. When we go to reconciliation, we receive the gift of God's grace to help us forgive others.

When we look at the world around us, we see people doing terrible evil things, and we see people doing beautiful, wonderful, loving things. What's the difference? It's usually a matter of openness to God's sanctifying grace in a person's life. Without the grace of God, the nicest person becomes capable of doing the most horrendous things.

*   *   *

Here's a summary of the forgiveness and healing exercise we recommend to couples.

Step One: Examination of conscience

Spend at least thirty minutes alone with God in prayer. Pray to God, expressing your desire that all hurt between you and your spouse would be healed. Ask God to show you the truth about the exact hurts you have caused your spouse in your marriage—whether it's by what you've said, by what you've done, or by what you haven't said or done. Think back to your dating days, engagement, and early marriage. When were you selfish, critical, insensitive, disrespectful, verbally or physically abusive, unsupportive, ungrateful, unfaithful, rejecting, or unforgiving?

It's important for you to think of the ways *you* have caused hurt and pain in the marriage. It's always easy to point out the ways your spouse has hurt you, but that's not what you're doing right now. It can lead to more problems, because it puts your spouse on the defensive. Avoid the urge to rationalize your own behavior, and don't blame your spouse for what you've done. Also, don't forget about the things you have failed to do that have contributed to the hurt and pain of your spouse.

Step Two: Confession

After you finish your lists, come together with your spouse. The husband should go first and recite from his list all the things he has done to cause hurt to his wife. You can start with a phrase like "I am sorry for the time I..." or "I am sorry for the way I..." After you've read the items from your list, ask your spouse for forgiveness. It's *very important* for the spouse to say the words "I forgive you."

Then the husband should ask if there is anything he might have forgotten that he needs to ask forgiveness for. If not, then the wife goes through the same confession, reading from her list and asking for forgiveness.

Step Three: Contrition

We must be truly sorry for the pain we have caused our spouse. That's easy to say but less easy to do. Remember, this isn't the time to think about what your spouse has done to you—that just gets you going in the wrong direction. We've come up with a prayer of contrition that's modeled on the Act of Contrition:

> O my [spouse's name], I am heartily sorry for having offended
> you.
> I detest all my sins, because of the way they hurt you,
> but most of all because they offended our God who is in you,
> who is all-good and deserving of all our love.
> I firmly resolve with the help of God's grace
> to not sin against you or intentionally hurt you
> and to avoid the near occasion of sin. Amen.

Avoid the temptation to place limits on your forgiveness. Specifically, avoid the temptation to punish your spouse with the silent treatment or by withholding love.

Step Four: Intention not to sin again

As in any good confession, we must try, to the best of our ability, coupled with God's grace, not to commit that sin again.

Step Five: Penance

Celebrate the sacrament of reconciliation as soon as possible.

This isn't exactly the process we went through, but because the sacrament of reconciliation proved to be effective for us, we added it as a final step in this exercise for couples. And it works.

*　　*　　*

We know that we're asking couples to do some serious work here. Many people have never spent a whole thirty minutes in prayer in their lives.

And it's not easy putting aside your resentments and trying to imagine what your spouse resents in you.

But you'll be amazed by how much this one exercise can change your marriage. Just hearing those words "I forgive you" can make everything different. One act of forgiveness can wash away years of resentment and hostility.

We appeared with another couple one time on a Catholic radio show to talk about healing and forgiveness after a marriage becomes severely troubled. The other couple said that forgiveness is a process, and it can take a while for couples to experience true forgiveness. We disagreed with them. Forgiveness and healing can take a long time when we try to do it with our *own* strength and on our *own* terms. It can happen in a moment when we humble ourselves and ask God to give us the grace to make it happen. If we're truly sorry and we're willing to let God's grace help us forgive, God will give us that grace. We've seen it happen too many times to dismiss it.

A few years ago we got a call on a Friday from a priest. He said he had a couple that needed to get in to see us right away. We met with the couple as soon as we could, and because the appointment was so rushed, we didn't have the information from our standard pre-coaching intake forms.

The couple sat on opposite ends of our couch, looking as cold toward each other as could be. I asked them what was going on, and the husband took the lead. "Well, I got the paternity test results Friday, telling me my new son isn't mine. His actual father is one of my wife's coworkers. And worse, if I hadn't found out about this when I did, my wife would have been with the father all this week on a business trip." Glaring right at me, he said, "Now, what are *you* going to do about this?"

I put on my poker face while I said a quick prayer for the Holy Spirit to guide my words. After a moment I calmly but firmly said, "I'm not a person to make assumptions, but I'm going to assume that because you're both here, there is a little love left in your relationship?"

They said yes, and so I said, "Then you need to use the love you have to open yourselves up to the grace of God so he can heal your relationship."

We had them complete the healing and forgiveness exercise before they came back to our next session. Two sessions later, they were sitting on our couch holding hands, giggling and chatting like newlyweds.

I looked at them with a big smile and said, "I know the answer to this question, but I need to hear it from your mouths. What do you think caused this change in your relationship?"

They smiled and looked at me and said, "The grace of God."

Think of that situation for a moment. A child, fathered in an adulterous relationship, is adopted by the husband who was cheated on. Only God can fill someone with enough love to do that. But God *can* fill you with that love. You just need to ask him for it.

This isn't the only miracle we've seen happen between husbands and wives because they were willing to forgive each other. That's why we don't think of this forgiveness and healing exercise as just a one-time thing. We encourage the couples we coach to make this just the *first* time they do the forgiveness and healing exercise. They should keep doing it for the rest of their lives. We challenge them to ask their spouse at the end of the day, "Is there anything I've done to you today I need to ask forgiveness for?"

What would happen to your marriage if you and your spouse did that every day? Your marriage would quickly become amazing—just the way ours did when we experienced God's forgiveness and healing in our marriage.

We hold our coaching clients accountable to totally forgiving their spouses for past offenses. Once they've completed the forgiveness and healing exercise, we don't let them bring up past hurts or issues. We must allow God to help us *totally* forgive our spouses for what they've done.

Is that hard? Of course it is. Jesus taught us that kind of forgiveness, not because he wanted to make things hard for us but because he knew that not forgiving ultimately makes our lives much harder. God will forgive even the worst sinner who comes to him with a contrite heart asking forgiveness. We need to do the same, and yet it's not possible for us on our own. Always remember that for God, everything is possible (see Matthew 19:26; Mark 10:27).

There will be times when your spouse is in the wrong and hasn't come to understand it yet. There will be times when you just can't imagine how a person could be so insensitive. Those are the times when you need to be faithful and pray even harder—for your spouse to open up to God's love and for yourself, for a spirit of forgiveness.

Yes, it's hard work. But your relationship can be *amazing* when you live it God's way.

Before you go on...
• In what ways have you offended your spouse?
• Are you willing to ask forgiveness? If not, what is holding you back?
• What habits have you fallen into that hurt your marriage?
• If you were really going to change yourself—not your spouse, but yourself—to make your marriage better, where would you start?

Do Something!

WHEN JULIE AND I QUIT our jobs and pulled away from everything that was leading us in the wrong direction, we thought we were headed the right way for the first time in a long time. But of course, we still had to live somehow. We tried various ways to bring in money. The important thing was that we were going to be together, working through our problems instead of running away from them, putting our relationship first instead of putting money first.

We started doing some consulting work with a law firm and a restaurant and doing marketing promotion at a couple of different nightclubs, creating and placing radio spots for them and that sort of thing. For a while we thought that was going to be our new life. Then a friend who had the marketing rights to a weight-loss energy supplement—we'd met him in the network-marketing world, so he knew our sales ability— called and said, "Hey, guys, I was wondering if you could help me set up some retail outlets. You know, buy from us wholesale, and resell to the outlets."

We were still go-getters. In probably two weeks we had fourteen different retail locations set up—pharmacies, health clubs, places like that. These supplements were selling like hotcakes. About a month later, our friend called back and said, "Hey, we have an idea for this concession trailer."

And pretty soon we had a bright red, five-by-eight concession trailer with the supplement logo on it. Julie negotiated a land lease at a bowling alley that was located at a very busy intersection. We paid five hundred dollars a month to park our trailer there, and we sold the pills from it. We were taking a big leap of faith. Was it possible to make a living this way?

One advantage of the job was that it involved a lot of free time. I'd spend literally eight hours a day in that trailer, reading the *Catechism*, my Bible, encyclicals, and all kinds of other books. I made a sort of deal with God. (I think we all do that when we really want something or when we're really worried about something.) My deal with God was that, if he allowed the sales to be OK, I would continue to read and study.

Well, the sales were good enough, so I kept studying.

After about three months of doing that, one evening I was packing up the trailer, and I *literally* heard a voice say, "You need to do something with this knowledge you've been learning."

Imagine me in that trailer, all alone, looking around for this voice. It was an internal voice. It wasn't a distinct voice. But I heard it.

So I packed up and went home, and I told Julie, "You're not going to believe this, but we're going to have to sell the trailer."

"What do you mean?" I think she said that a lot in the first few months of putting our lives back together.

I said, "I know it sounds weird, but while I was packing up today, I felt as if God was telling me that I have to start doing something with this knowledge that I'm learning."

She was a bit upset about that. We were probably retailing $3500 to $4000 a month in that trailer, and now I was telling her we had to put this stuff away and do something different. "We just started getting a steady stream of income coming in here!" she objected. "We can't sell the trailer!"

And I said, "I know it sounds funny, but you've got to trust me."

*   *   *

By then we had started going to daily Mass as often as possible. I remember that this conversation with Julie happened on a Tuesday, because Mass on Tuesday was in the evening. I don't remember what the Gospel was that night, but I do remember hearing the priest say in the homily, "There are many times in our lives when we feel that God is calling us and asking us to do something. But it's unfortunate that our trust and our faith in God are not strong enough that we can follow through and do what he's asking."

He went on from there. But at that point I looked over at Julie, and she looked at me, and she mouthed, "OK, we can sell the trailer."

So we went to see our friend and explained the situation to him. Not only did we give him the trailer back, we said that he could keep the money we had paid into it. We just wanted out so that we could pursue what we felt God was calling us to do. We went back to some sales and marketing consulting, working with another restaurant.

By then we had started attending some family-advocacy classes on behalf of the diocese of Austin. That was how we got to know Janice, the family life director there. We talked with her about the idea we had of putting together a nonprofit to work with married couples. We were calling it The Alexander House.

Well, after about five of those classes, Janice called Julie one day and said, "Look, I'm having major back problems. I'm gong to have to quit, effective immediately, and I'm trying to find somebody who can fill in at the office. Would you be willing to fill in as a coordinator?"

So Julie started a new job in the Family Life Office. I would go with her, and after a couple of months, the director of the pastoral center decided it would be great to have a couple in this position. She said to me, "Why don't you come and work out of the office as well? We'll back-date your pay to when Julie started, and you can also work on your non-profit."

That's what I did. Once again we were working together—but this time we were doing something really worthwhile.

*   *   *

All this time I was still reading and studying and learning. I had so much to catch up on!

One day I was sitting in the office, after Julie had gone home, and I ran across the encyclical *Humanae Vitae.* And that's how I started to learn about the Church's teaching and position on contraception and sterilization. For the first time I understood that married love was meant to be *fruitful.*

I learned that our love for each other grows more fruitful as we deepen our trust and open ourselves to each other. The healing that comes from both forgiving and being forgiven is vital to this trust and openness. Without it we will guard our hearts and never let our spouse close enough to us to let love grow.

All fruitfulness requires a total trust in God, because we know deep down we don't have what it takes to support what comes from the fruits of our love. Opening ourselves up and trusting more deeply means risk-ing more. Greater risk brings with it the potential for greater hurt. Our threshold for risk is only as big as our faith in God.

But our married love *wasn't* fruitful. I'd had that little operation to make sure it wouldn't be. I had not thought at all about the implications for my faith when I did it, but now I was suddenly confronted with the reality of what I'd done.

I called Julie on the phone and said, "Hey, I'll be home in a minute. I hate to leave the office, but we've got a problem."

She said, "What do you mean, we've got a problem?"

I said, "I'll explain it when I get there."

When I got home, I told her what I had just been reading and what I had suddenly realized about that vasectomy I'd had after our second child was born. Yes, we had been ignorant of Church teaching on this topic, but a whole lot of selfishness had fueled our decision to let a doctor mutilate my reproductive system. I used to tell others that I had been "fixed," until one day my sister-in-law gently reminded me that I had been broken. I never used that term again.

The damage had been done ten years before. Now we were beginning to understand how this evil had impacted our marriage. As we looked back to where things had gone wrong, we found that many of our problems had started *after* the vasectomy. I believe that once I cut God out of my life and usurped his power to give life to our marriage when we came together in the marital embrace, I also cut out some of the grace of the sacrament of marriage—the very grace that could have saved us.

Now, I must say that reversing a sterilization is not something that the Church requires you to do. However, as I prayed, I discerned God calling me to do this. I wanted to be restored to what He had created me to be in the first place.

Before you go on...

• Many of us talk to God, in prayer or even more casually. But do you ever *listen* to God?

• What do you think God is trying to tell you right now?

Undoing the Damage

·

·

·

·

·

·

WHEN GREG CAME HOME AND told me what he'd read in this encyclical from Pope Paul VI—how contraception was wrong and sterilization was against God's will—well, I was shocked. "What are we going to do?" I asked. You have to remember that, even though we'd begun to study Catholic teaching, we were still pretty ignorant.

So we went to confession. Greg was shaking like crazy when the priest walked in, he said. He started telling the priest what we were going through, that he had been sterilized, and now we'd found out what the Church teaches about that. What could we do?

The priest was very understanding, of course. He was happy we were learning about our Catholic faith, and he told Greg that he was not in any serious trouble. Due to the fact that we were not in full knowledge of the Church's teaching at that time, Greg could not be held accountable. Father also said that, because a reversal procedure is serious surgery, in which one of the possible outcomes is death, the Church would not require Greg to have the sterilization reversed.

And then he said, "Go and sin no more." We were OK with that.

A few weeks later my mom sent us a flyer about a marriage conference that would be held in Denver. Now, we had always wanted to do a seminar for our nonprofit, which by this time we had named The Alexander House. So we asked for more information on how the sponsors were going to run it, and we decided to go to the conference as well.

A priest gave the first talk, entitled "God's Plan for Marriage." It was about all the things that we had been learning and had begun to incorporate into our marriage. We were sitting in the front row with my brother and his wife, nodding in affirmation. We knew all this stuff now!

The next talk was by Christopher West: "God's Gift of Sacramental Sex." As he started talking, we were still nodding. Then he came to the issues of contraception and sterilization and explained how they violate the fruitful and total aspect of the marriage.

Greg and I looked at each other. Despite what the priest had told Greg when we went to confession, we couldn't help feeling, *We're in trouble.*

After the talk my brother pretty bluntly said to Greg, "So, what are you going to do about your vasectomy?"

My brother and sister-in-law were the only ones on my side of the family who knew that Greg had had a vasectomy. Even though, when I was growing up, I had never really heard the word *contraception* and never heard about sterilization, for some reason Greg and I both knew that it was something we shouldn't tell my parents. I still can't figure out where that came from, maybe subconsciously knowing, in my heart, it was wrong.

But we had told my brother and his wife. And now he was all over Greg, saying, "Hey, you've *got* to get that reversed. You're jeopardizing your soul."

Greg responded, "Hey, you know, I've gone to confession, and the priest told me we were fine."

"Well, you know," my brother said, "if it's a matter of money, we'll dig in our pockets, and we'll help you pay for this."

I was really surprised at his generosity. He must have thought it was something very important.

Greg answered, "That's not the issue. I'm OK. I'm feeling good."

But he wasn't feeling good. I know, because he started talking about it as we were driving back to Texas. It was obviously on his mind.

"Look, Julie," he said, "I'm having a hard time with this. I can't work in a family life office, and I can't continue to pursue The Alexander House."

"What do you mean?" I asked.

We had given our lives to our apostolate. We didn't know exactly where it was going yet, but we had quit our jobs and given up on all the material things we used to think were so necessary. We were committed. Now he wanted to quit?

"There's no way I could stand in front of people and teach and preach how they should be when I'm not compliant," he explained.

And again I asked, "So what are we going to do?"

"Well, first," he said, "I think we need to pray."

So we did pray, right there in the car. What Greg prayed was something like this: "Father, based on what the Church teaches, and based on what we heard at this conference, I do feel that I am in good graces with you. However, I feel something different inside. And if that's you telling me that I need to do something different, I'm going to need you to show me a sign."

*   *   *

A week later, back in Austin, I was rearranging the books on the shelves in the office, and at random I pulled out a little book called *Physicians Healed.* It's a compilation of stories of doctors who used to prescribe the pill and other kinds of contraception but, because of their conversion, no longer do so. I looked on the back cover, and it was from the Natural Family Planning Office. Right there on the book was the name and number of the director.

Right away I called. For some reason I held back on what I was really up to. I didn't actually lie, but I didn't exactly tell the whole truth.

"Hi, this is Julie," I told the person on the other end of the line. "My husband, Greg, and I are new in the Family Life Office, and *just in case* we get people coming to the door wanting information about reversal doctor referrals, do you happen to have any?"

The man on the other end answered, "Well, there are two doctors here in Austin. I'll give you their numbers. I've got a third doctor in New Braunfels that I don't know anything about, but feel free to have his information."

I hung up, and right away I called the first two doctors. I got their answering machines. So I called that third doctor in New Braunfels, and I got his receptionist, and she patched me straight through to Dr. Leverett.

I gave him the same story: We're in the Family Life Office in Austin, we're looking for reversal doctor information, do you have any information you could send us?

"I'll put something in the mail," he answered. "But in the meantime you can take a look at my website, www.reversals.com."

So as soon as I got off the phone, Greg immediately went to the website. It starts right out with Scripture; it has wonderful testimonies, beautiful pictures of what they call "reversal babies," and more.

He was as enthusiastic as I was. "You've got to call this guy back and get an appointment," he said. "I think this is the guy who's going to do my reversal."

So I called the doctor back and talked with the receptionist. "Hi, I'm Julie. I just spoke with Dr. Leverett. I'm calling back to see if I can get an appointment."

The nurse said, "Well, I just had a cancellation for tomorrow at 11:30. Can you make it?"

I took the appointment. But meanwhile Greg was on the computer trying to see what reversal surgery costs. (In the military, you know, the vasectomy was free.) What he found was that it cost anywhere from six to twenty thousand dollars, depending on complications, whether it's done in the hospital, whether the doctor uses local or general anesthetic, and so on.

When he told me that, I said, "Well, that's it. That's God's sign."

"What do you mean?" Greg asked.

"Well, you asked God for a sign when we were coming back from Denver," I explained. "Now he's giving it to you. We can't afford six thousand dollars, let alone twenty thousand. That's God's sign that we can't do this, so we might as well forget it."

I think I underestimated how much the vasectomy was bothering Greg, now that he knew the Church's teaching about sterilization, and how much he wanted to have it reversed.

"Look," he said, "we have this appointment tomorrow. Let's at least keep the appointment, talk to the doctor, and see what he has to say."

So the next day we showed up. The doctor was a bit surprised when the nurse took us back to his office. "Julie Alexander—didn't I just talk to you? I promised to send you some information. Is the mail not fast enough?"

I laughed. "Well, yeah, it's fast enough, but we want to talk to you about our story."

We gave him an abridged version, of course, but we told him the important parts—how we were on the brink of divorce, how we were now in a family life office and creating this apostolate to start working with couples, and how Greg was uncomfortable because of the vasectomy he'd had.

Since we'd been so candid with him, Dr. Leverett shared his own conversion story with us. Then he took us on a tour around his office—

he had an in-house operating suite. We went by a wall where all the pictures of his reversal babies were, children of couples who had conceived post-reversal. I watched Greg as he looked at the pictures. I knew exactly what was in his mind. To be honest, I wanted it too. But the money!

We got back to his office, and Dr. Leverett said, "So what do you guys think?"

Greg said, "I want to do this. How soon can I do it?"

Dr. Leverett flipped through his calendar. "Well, I've got next Tuesday at 7:50 AM. Will that work?"

Immediately Greg said, "Yeah, we'll take it."

"Wait a minute!" I interrupted. Things seemed to be getting out of control. "We've done our research. We totally trust your ability, but we also know what these things cost. Unless we can make some kind of payment plan, we're not going to be able to pay for this."

Dr. Leverett sat there for a second. He leaned back in his big leather chair with his hands behind his back, silent for a moment. Then he leaned forward.

"You know," he said, "I admire the heck out of you two guys. Not only about where you've been but also because of where you're going. Especially your ministry. So I think I want to make an investment. I tell you what: Come see me next Tuesday at 7:50, and bring me five hundred dollars."

Well, we'd quit our jobs, and we weren't bringing in much money. And by some wild coincidence, all we had in our bank account was five hundred dollars. My natural thought was, "That's the last five hundred bucks we have."

But we did it. Greg was right. There was no way we were going to let five hundred dollars stand in the way of getting our lives right with God again.

*   *   *

"I'm one up on old Humpty Dumpty," Greg said as we were coming home from the operation.

I laughed. "What are you talking about?"

"Well, you know the nursery rhyme. All the king's horses and all the king's men couldn't put him together again. But all it took for me was Dr. Leverett."

Nine months after that, I gave Greg a Father's Day card. I watched him open it, because I'd slipped a little something into it.

"Whose is this?" he asked incredulously, holding up a positive pregnancy test.

"It's the neighbor's," I shouted back in exasperation. "Whose in the world do you think it is?"

Before you go on...

• What are the vices that keep you from experiencing greatness in your marriage?

• Are you able to openly communicate to your spouse the struggles that you have in your life and in your marriage?

• Are you open to life?

Building the Apostolate

ABOUT NINE MONTHS AFTER, JULIE gave me that Father's Day card, we had little Katharine. We call her the incarnation of our reconciliation. We named her after St. Katharine Drexel, who was canonized about four months before little Katharine was born. She was the first of what our older children call our second family.

If you looked at our bio, you already know that we have seven kids. I remember back in the old days how we used to shuffle our two kids off to day care or anywhere else we could so we could keep on doing what we thought was really important, which was bringing in more money. It's amazing how much we sacrificed because we thought we were going to find our happiness in the next *thing*. And now we're at the point where we don't care to leave our kids at all. We don't care to be away from each other, because our joy is found in being together, sharing our time, sharing our moments.

No wonder our older kids say it's our second family—because we really are different people!

*   *   *

About a year before Katharine was born, The Alexander House hosted its first workshop. The presenters were all people who had played a role in our lives as we made our way back to the Church, starting with the priest who challenged us to learn God's plan for marriage, and ending with the doctor who performed my reversal. It was awesome watching others receive in one day what had taken us about a year and a half to discover.

Two weeks before this event, I had another strange encounter. I was in the bathroom one morning getting dressed, and again I heard a voice. This time it said, "I want you to talk to my people." And I immediately dropped to my knees.

At that moment Julie walked in, and she said that my face was as white as a sheet. And I heard again, "I want you to talk to my people." So I said to this voice (internally), "What do you want me to do?" and then I heard, "You need to pray and go to confession."

I do not share this too often. In fact, if someone had told me this story before it happened to me, I would have said, "Yeah, right." But it's true.

I didn't know what to do, so I called the priest who had challenged us to read and study, and I said, "Father, something strange happened to me this morning. I want to share it with you." And I told him about the incident.

"Well," he said, "the only thing I can gather from that is, if God is really calling you and wanting to use you, then you're going to have to remain a pure vessel. You're going to have to go to confession. Going to confession purges your soul and makes you an empty vessel to be filled with God's grace. And you must pray to stay in communication with God and allow him to guide you."

Whether we know it or not, God does have a plan for us in our lives and in our marriages. However, if we aren't in communication with him, how are we to know what he is asking from us?

So I went to confession, and I've tried to keep the lines of communication open to heaven ever since. I'm sure that voice was right. Without that purification, and without that constant help from God, I'm sure we could never have done anything in our apostolate. We didn't have the strength to do it ourselves. God had to give us the strength.

*   *   *

We started our apostolate small, just doing informal talks at our church. At those informal talks we would ask couples, "What do you think is God's plan for marriage?" It was kind of weird just to say those words, thinking, *These people are going to think we're crazy.*

And you should have seen the blank stares! *God* has a plan for *marriage?* What do you mean? They looked so dumbfounded.

I remembered, that's where *we* were until a little while ago! We had no idea that there was a divine plan for marriage. We thought marriage was all about *us* and what *we* wanted. What did God have to do with it?

By the time we were through with the talk, these couples had been introduced to an amazing idea. And I know that for some of them it was a life-changing idea.

This was also a nerve-racking experience. When we began our apostolate, I told Julie that I would do anything but stand in front of people and speak. I was deathly afraid of public speaking. But I found that this wasn't so bad, because I was among some familiar faces.

So where would our apostolate go from here? It was Julie who took the next step.

We got a call one day from the adult education director at another parish. Julie answered the phone, and the woman at the other end said, "I've heard about the talks you've been giving. Do you guys have a workshop?"

And Julie said, "Sure, we have a workshop." She set a date. And *then* she came to me and said, "Hey, we got our first workshop."

"What are you talking about?" I answered, a little worried. "We don't have a workshop."

She said, "Well, we've got a date. You better come up with *something*."

So I did. And I think that's how our apostolate has operated till this day. We feel the call to do something, and *then* we figure out *how* to do it. We have to fully rely on God. It's quite a change from the old Greg and Julie, who had a plan for everything. But it has been part of learning to trust—learning to trust the Holy Spirit and learning to trust each other.

After the workshop Julie looked at me with tears in her eyes and said, "Do you know what you just did?"

I responded, "Yes, I made it through this terrifying experience."

Julie said quietly, in almost a whisper, "No, you were talking to his people."

*   *   *

That first workshop ended up being a big success. After it couples came up and said, "Hey, the workshop was great, but we need more individual attention. Do you work with couples?"

I took a page from Julie's book, and in my most confident voice I said, "Sure, we work with couples. When do you want to get started?" Obviously we didn't have a plan for working with couples, but we'd figure it out somehow along the way.

Initially we called it "marriage mentoring." We started advising couples by just sitting at a table and letting them dump on us, the way we had dumped our whole sad story on others. We'd sit there two or three hours, just listening to the stories going back and forth and back and forth. It was pretty draining sometimes, but we'd help them sort through their issues, and if they felt like donating afterward, they could.

We had been working in the Family Life Office and feeling a nudge to pray for direction. It started with wanting to spare any couple from going through the hell that we had put each other through. Then it was about assisting others in finding joy in their marriage. But it came down to leading others closer to Christ. If we could utilize what we had gone through to allow others to learn from our mistakes and realize that they need God in their lives and in their marriages, then we would be successful.

With this mindset it did not matter to us how we accomplished the task to lead others to the truth, the teachings of the Church, and ultimately to Christ. We were on fire for our faith and wanted to share that passion with anyone who came to us.

We desired nothing more than to remain open to the will of God, who had brought us out of the mess we were in and had led us to this point. We knew that everything we did had more to do with Christ dwelling in us than with us, so we prayed for grace and humility. We even discussed the idea that if God was calling us to forgo The Alexander House, we would be obedient, because we were adamant about fulfilling his plan for us.

We had an unexpected meeting with the new director of the Pastoral Center and a coworker. We were asked to pray and discern about working in the Family Life Office or pursuing our nonprofit. "We will give you a week to let us know," they said, and the meeting was over.

For me there was no doubt about what our decision would be. However, Julie was dismayed and in a little bit of a panic. When we arrived home, she cried like a baby and lamented to God, "We are doing this for you. Why would you allow this to happen?" Maybe this was God's way of closing a door so that we could go in the direction that he wanted.

That very evening we were scheduled to present a talk to the residents at a local maternity home. My first thought was that I was not in the mood to speak to some young women about their lives, when I wasn't exactly sure where mine was going to end up. But we kept our commitment and discovered a beauty in meeting with these unwed teenage mothers. We talked to them about relationships and chastity and prayer, and most importantly about God.

When we had concluded our session, I looked at Julie and said, "I feel that this is where we are supposed to be." Without hesitation she agreed.

The next day we contacted the owners of the maternity home and spoke with them about the possibility of becoming house parents. Within a couple of weeks, we and our three kids were moving in. Feeling the call to possibly make this our lifelong position, once again we thought that we did not need to continue with The Alexander House. We put it on the back burner.

In the process of cleaning out our house, we planned a small garage sale to dispose of the items that we no longer needed. The day started off cloudy and soon became rainy, which changed our outdoor plans. We put the items in the front room and allowed customers to come in and purchase what was for sale. People began walking through the house and bargaining with us for items that were not on the inventory. Before we knew it, our house was cleaned out.

As each item left the premises, we felt lighter and lighter. We had a few things left, but now it was manageable to rent a very small truck and move everything that we owned to our new location.

Quickly we realized that keeping our house was not smart economically. We were never there, so why have mortgage payments? We decided without hesitation to put the house on the market.

The house never sold. Julie was especially frustrated that we were stuck with this house that we did not need and that was taking what little money we had. Then we received a phone call from a couple we knew; they were in need of a place to rent. Our house just happened to be down the street from the woman's mother, and the location was ideal for them.

*   *   *

During our time at the maternity home we served over sixty girls. The majority came from broken homes and had grown up without father figures. I soon became the father figure for all of them. Our time was consumed by conversations with these young women, helping them find dignity and worth within themselves.

We kept a schedule for every day that included devotions in the chapel with the residents. One morning Julie conducted the morning devotion alone, and when she came back from the chapel, she was in tears. She said to me, "I cannot do this anymore. I feel as if the grace is gone. I am tired, and I do not think I have what it takes anymore."

I replied with, "What do you propose we do? We have nowhere to go, no job to support us. And there is no way The Alexander House can provide what we need to survive. I'm afraid that I would not be able to support our family." We had $250 in The Alexander House account, and we had no plan as to how we could make the apostolate a full-time endeavor.

We tabled the discussion and decided to go to Mass. Fr. Brian McMaster walked in and asked us to recite the entrance antiphon. It was Jeremiah 17:7–8:

> Blessed is the man who trusts in the LORD,
>> whose hope is the LORD.
> He is like a tree planted beside the waters
>> that stretches out its roots to the stream:
> It fears not the heat when it comes,
>> its leaves stay green;
> In the year of drought it shows no distress,
>> but still bears fruit. (*NAB*)

I turned to Julie and asked, "Did you hear that?"

"Hear what?" she said.

"That reading?"

I repeated the verse and then immediately dropped to my knees. Julie had no idea what I was doing. I looked at the crucifix and prayed, "Father, why do I find it so hard to trust you, when I know what it is that you are asking of me? If you are calling us to pursue The Alexander House on a full-time basis—I'm yours."

I sat back in the pew, and instantaneously I felt a warmth come over my body. It felt as if God gave me a big hug, assuring me that all would be well. "That is it; we are gone!" I said to Julie.

She said, "We can't leave Mass."

I said, "No, but we are going to do The Alexander House full-time."

I didn't know how we were going to make it happen. The one thing I was certain of was that this is what God wanted of us. I knew that he would provide.

*   *   *

Immediately upon our arrival back at the maternity home, we scheduled a meeting with the owners and told them of our decision. They were not thrilled. We were gone within a few days.

Julie wondered what she had started. She thought, *We are going to be homeless, as we have nowhere to go.* Yet even though it seemed as if we were getting ready to enter into a world of chaos, we both felt a huge sense of peace.

As I began packing, I received a phone call. It was Carlos. Julie and I had coached him and his wife, but subsequently they had divorced. He was distraught because he had just learned that his ex-wife, who had remarried, was now pregnant. He needed to speak to someone.

I said in an unsettled voice, "Carlos, I'm having some issues of my own. I don't even know where I will be living next week. But when I get situated, I promise to give you a call."

With excitement in his voice, he responded, "Hey, look, I am a single guy with a four-bedroom home. Why don't you all come stay here with me until you get situated?"

We were so thankful for his offer. We did not want to be an inconvenience, but we couldn't move back into our own house because it was still rented out. So we moved in with Carlos. Julie and I slept on an air mattress, while our three children shared a room with a double bed.

As time went on, nothing seemed to be materializing in terms of The Alexander House. I was starting to get discouraged, because here I was in my forties, and I did not know how I was going to provide for my family. I finally broke down and got a local paper.

I was sitting on the couch browsing through the want ads when Julie walked downstairs. When she saw me, she immediately started to cry. She walked over to the window, and she managed to get a few words out between sniffles: "Is this what we left for—just to get another job? God, we are doing this for you—why don't you help us?"

I knew she was confused and concerned. We talked about how we could not give up on what we felt God was asking us to do.

*   *   *

We had an appointment with a priest to let him know our plans of working in The Alexander House full-time. When the meeting was over, Julie and I noticed a tear running down his face. We stood up to give him a hug, and he said, "Thank you! I cannot believe how much faith the two of you have. It is nice to see a couple believe in something so much that you are willing to give up everything you own to make it happen." Little did he know that he was the one who put wind in our sails to give us the courage to continue on the journey.

Once we got back to Carlos's house, I noticed that we had two missed calls on the answering machine. Julie hit the button, and the first message was from a producer with EWTN. He asked if we would consider being on a show called *Life on the Rock*, to talk about marriage and dating for young adults.

The next call was from a gentleman from Arkansas. His voice was very confident and assuring, and we listened several times to his message: "I heard about the work that you all are doing for marriages, and I would like to offer you a challenge grant. You raise ten thousand dollars and I will match it."

They say that when it rains it pours, and it felt as though the floodgates were opening, until we received another call that same week. The couple that had been renting our home was moving out because they had bought a new house. We were excited to get back into our home, but the sobering thought of how we were going to make the payments lingered in our minds. But again, we knew that God would provide.

So there we were, December 17, a week before Christmas, moving back into our empty home. No furniture, no Christmas tree, and definitely no money for presents. Trying to figure out what we were going to do for the kids that Christmas was leading us down another road of despair. But a few days later, there was a knock on the door.

Julie was a bit hesitant about flinging the door open and exposing our empty house. So she opened it slowly, allowing just enough space to peek out and see who it was. To our surprise it was a dear friend from church, greeting us with a tree, boxes of ornaments, and presents for the children that covered the porch. (The kids had more presents that Christmas than they had ever had.)

I looked at her with a humbled face and said, "You know, a few years ago my pride would have been too great to take this gift, but now I know it's God's way of thanking us by sending us an angel so that we can have a merry Christmas. I thank you."

We had disclosed the challenge grant offer to only a few people, but checks began coming in from everywhere—from family members, friends, old acquaintances, and never-before-heard-of supporters. It was incredible!

A few days after Christmas, a friend who belonged to our parish called. He and his family were in Houston for Christmas, and his son had fallen ill. He did not want the rest of the relatives to get sick, so they were returning home. He wanted to stop by and drop off an end-of-the-year donation.

Julie was so anxious to get the envelope that she practically ripped it from his hand. She tore it open, and the amount of the check took us $46 over $10,000. And this was on the Feast of the Holy Family.

We will never forget that pivotal moment. God was speaking to us loud and clear. Literally in six weeks, we went from having $250 in The Alexander House account to having $20,250 in the bank. This was enough inspiration to allow us to forge forward, no matter what obstacles might try to prevent us from continuing to strengthen marriages (and believe me, there have been many, too many, to mention here).

*   *   *

The journey has been an amazing ride, a rollercoaster of emotions and struggles. At one point we were given nine and a half acres in Austin, and an architect donated his time to draw up the plans. Shortly after the completion of the blueprint for one of two planned buildings, we felt God calling us to move to San Antonio!

Through all of this we have been confident that the God who called us to do his work will see it through. We are mere instruments who vow to stay open to his will and his direction, no matter where it takes us.

I don't mind saying that, despite all that we have experienced with God, we still waver from time to time. This serves to remind us of the fact that without him we can do nothing. We pray daily for the understanding and the grace to do all of our work in order to glorify God.

Melissa Johnson, a good friend of Julie from high school, once told her that our walk with God is sometimes like standing on the top of a mountain, and when it is time to take that next step, he will either be there to catch you or give you wings to fly. There are times when we are tested, but those trials are always opportunities to grow stronger and to allow God to show us his love and mercy.

Before you go on...

- Do you make plans for your marriage, or do you take things as they come?
- Are you open to allowing God to work in your marriage?
- Do you invite God into all areas of your marriage, that he may provide the grace that you need?

There Are Always Lessons to Learn

So HERE WE ARE, GREG and I, with seven children and an apostolate that's grown far beyond what we ever expected.

Do we have an easy life? Well, no. Bad things happen to everyone sometimes. I had so much trouble delivering our sixth child that, a while later, I nearly died from a heart attack. We've had money troubles, health problems, and just plain bad luck. Sometimes we stub our toes, and it hurts like anything.

That's what it's like being human. In this imperfect and sinful world, even living your life according to God's plan doesn't get you a free pass. You still have to suffer sometimes.

Greg

Saturday, October 25, 2008, two months after we had our sixth child (Javan), Julie, with a chilling tone in her voice, summoned me to our bedroom. "Greg, I think I'm having a heart attack!" she exclaimed. Thinking, *No way!* I suggested that she lie down while I prepared breakfast for the kids.

I have to tell you that three days prior she had experienced a pain in her chest and in her jaw. Unbeknownst to us, these are the classic symptoms of a female having a heart attack. I had suggested she do what my dad had always prescribed for us when we had an ache or pain: take a hot bath.

While she was in the bath, I had gone online to see if I could identify what these symptoms could be pointing to. Several sites suggested that it could be a heart attack, but if so the symptoms would include cold sweats and pain shooting down the left arm. There was no pain in the arm or cold sweat, so we just dismissed the whole episode, especially when she began to feel better.

Julie called out again. "I think I'm going to die!"

Nonchalantly I made my way to the bedroom, only to find her slumping over in a pool of sweat. She said that she had pain shooting down her left arm. Not even thinking about calling 911, I got everyone in the car, took the older kids to a friend's house, and proceeded to the emergency room with Julie and the baby.

Julie was hesitant to go to the hospital. She thought she might just have something like indigestion. The attendant took her information and her history. Julie had to have an EKG. Then we returned to the waiting area, figuring we'd be out of there in a few moments.

The doctor called us back into the exam room. There she explained that the EKG didn't look right. She thought that maybe the new tech on staff had crossed the wires or something, and she ordered the test to be repeated. This time we didn't get sent back to the waiting area.

Within minutes the doctor rushed back and in a low and stern voice whispered, "Mr. Alexander, I don't want to alarm you, but your wife is experiencing a heart attack." Numbed by her words, I looked at Julie, thinking, *How can this be? I'm the one with the bad cholesterol and triglycerides that are off the chart. This just can't be.*

The doctor made me aware of the fact that they were prepping the heart cath lab, and the cardiologist was on his way. Not long after that, they were wheeling Julie off to the cath lab, and I was left standing there, dazed and confused, with my two-month-old in my arms.

I pulled out my cell phone and immediately started calling all of our immediate family. Everyone was just as confused as I was. My mom, who was at a Bible study, asked the group for prayers and then made her way to the hospital. We sat there for what seemed like hours, and then we got the call to head to the cath lab.

As we walked in, I could see that the images on the screen didn't look right. The doctor made matters worse when he confirmed that Julie was indeed having a heart attack—but that her heart was fine. Apparently she had experienced a spontaneous dissection of her left anterior descending coronary artery. He determined that this must have been happening gradually, for quite some time, as the films illustrated that her body had already started growing collateral arteries to try to get blood to her heart. (It is amazing how the body tries to heal itself. If only we could be so quick to move when we find that our soul is in need of healing!)

Of course, the only questions on my mind were, *What does this all mean?* and *What is her prognosis?* Because her body was already trying to heal itself, the cardiologist elected not to do anything surgical; that would have halted the healing process. He also said that doing anything invasive might collapse the already weakened arterial system. His decision was to wait.

Wait? I thought to myself. *How can you just wait and do nothing?* The words *second opinion* were swirling in my mind, but I had a hunch that this man knew what he was doing. Away we went to ICU. There Julie would later experience some internal bleeding that warranted a CAT scan to identify the source.

After a long day at the hospital, I made my way home that night to do my own research, as the doctor had not been able to give me much information. Apparently Julie's condition was a fairly new one, and the medical people didn't know a lot about what actually caused it and what was the best approach for treatment. Once again I made my way to the Internet to see what I could find out.

Every study I found made me more depressed, because all of the information presented came from women postmortem. I plopped down on the bed, looking over at Julie's empty pillow, then rolled onto my back and looked at the ceiling with tears streaming down my face—pleading with God not to let me go to bed alone for the rest of my life. *After all we have been through, but more importantly after all we have survived, I can't lose her now.* I got up and started sending out e-mails explaining Julie's situation and asking for intercessory prayer specifically through John Paul II; I just felt that he was the "go to" guy.

I made my way back to the hospital on Sunday, and things were much the same as the day before. Julie was in a whole lot of pain, and there was nothing that I could do. Her pain meds were maxed out, and they didn't appear to come even close to bringing any relief for her. We talked and prayed and kept our focus on all of the things we knew that we had to finish for God—*together.* I stayed with Julie until 3:30 AM, when she forced me to go home and get some sleep.

I returned Monday morning at 8:30 AM. To my surprise, I saw my bride lying there as if nothing had ever happened. In amazement I said, "Don't take this wrong, but for someone who just had a heart attack, you sure look pretty good." I continued, "How is the pain in your back?"

"It's gone," she replied.

"What about in your chest?"

And she said, "I have none."

We shared Julie's situation with the nurse. The doctor was contacted, and we were told that he had requested another heart catheterization to be performed that afternoon.

Eagerly I walked downstairs as they wheeled Julie to the cath lab. I gave the tech my cell number so he could call me when she was on her way back to her room.

I had to go see the older kids, since they had not seen me at all since Saturday. When I saw their beautiful little faces, all I could think of was what I would tell them if their mommy was not going to come back home. They were too little to be allowed to visit in the ICU, so I decided to videotape them saying hello to Mom, and I would do the same with her so they could see her as well. I promised myself that I would do this every day until she came home. Ah, the power of positive thinking.

I failed to make it back in time to see Julie after the study. But Jimmy, the tech, gave me a call and told me to go to her room, and the doctor would be there soon. Well, we waited for an hour, and no doc. Two hours, and no doc. The staff called and paged, but nothing. He was nowhere to be found, and the suspense was killing me.

All of a sudden I noticed Jimmy walking across the ICU floor, and I called him over. I asked him to tell me the results of the study, and with a confused look on his face, he said, "You mean the doc has not made his way up here yet to see you?" I told him no. He then said, "Man, I thought for sure he would have made a beeline to her room after the study."

I quickly asked, "So is that a good thing or a bad thing?"

Jimmy reassured me, "It's a good thing. I've been doing this work for fifteen years, and never have I seen a dissected artery not only come back together on its own but reconstitute blood flow. Brother, whatever you guys are doing, keep doing it, because your wife is getting blood to her heart!"

God does answer prayers; he answered mine that day. And I'm sure glad that he didn't answer Julie's.

Later that day she said to me, "Honey, I said a prayer last night."

"Really," I said, "what was your prayer?"

Casually she responded, "Oh, I told God that if it took me dying to further our apostolate, it would be OK."

Immediately I said, "No more praying for you. I'm the spiritual leader of this family, and from now on I will lead the prayers. In fact, that was a pretty selfish prayer."

Julie also told me that she had felt a deep longing inside for God, and she had cried as never before—because all she wanted was to see and be with him.

Let me tell you, even a heart attack is nothing compared to the misery we put ourselves through before we learned to put God first. I know that God placed a desire for him inside of us, and that he wants us to experience those same feelings toward each other. Again, God has given us each other to learn to love as he loves—freely, totally, faithfully, and fruitfully.

Can you say that you love your spouse that way? More importantly, do you love God that way?

Think of how Christ called his disciples. They all had important things to do. But he told them to put the kingdom of God first:

> To another he said, "Follow me." But he said, "Lord, let me first go and bury my father." But he said to him, "Leave the dead to bury their own dead; but as for you, go and proclaim the kingdom of God." (Luke 9:59–60)

> [Christ said,] "He who loves father or mother more than me is not worthy of me; and he who loves son or daughter more than me is not worthy of me." (Matthew 10:37)

Does that mean we're not supposed to love our families? Of course not, but we are called to place God and Christ as number one in our lives, above all else.

Julie

I recognized an enormous longing for God when I was in the hospital. It seemed as though nothing else mattered more than strengthening my relationship with God and having a good relationship with others —especially with Greg.

The good news from the doctor that I was able to go home was followed by a big disappointment. At the time of my heart attack, we did not have health insurance, simply because we could not afford it. About a week after getting home from the hospital, I received a disturbing phone call from the billing department. A woman who was determined to accomplish her job proceeded to ask how I wanted to pay my $81,000 hospital bill. "Would you like to pay $4,682 per month, or would $2,341 work better?" she asked carelessly.

I chuckled. "How about $10 per month?"

She snickered and asked, "What did you say?"

I repeated my response. I told her our story and about The Alexander House, in hopes of getting a bit of sympathy from her. I guess it didn't make any difference, because she then said, "Can I ask you a question?"

"Sure," I said.

"What were you thinking?"

"What do you mean? I wanted to live. I went to the hospital closest to my house."

"There are hospitals downtown for people like you," she rudely commented, referring to people without health insurance.

She literally left me speechless. I felt hurt, confused, and a little panicked about what we were going to do.

Her next comment assured me that she cared nothing about my situation. "You know, maybe you should play the lotto."

I responded, "I've played before, and it doesn't work."

She ended our verbal joust with, "Better luck next time."

I was shocked and devastated at the lack of respect I received from this woman. I immediately called Greg, and he could tell by my shaking voice that something was really wrong. After I explained things to him, he too was shocked about the treatment I had received. But he calmly responded, "Call the guy that checked us into the hospital. He said that if we needed anything, don't hesitate to call him."

When I was admitted to the hospital, I explained our story to this young man, and he had been very inspired by what we did. But I dialed the number thinking, *What can this kid do for me? He just works in admissions, and I'm sure that he doesn't have any pull there.*

He answered immediately. Without hesitation I explained my disappointment and, more importantly, my fear of not being able to pay what was owed to the hospital. His quick response to my dilemma gave me hope. He said that he had an idea, and I should call him back in fifteen minutes.

I don't think I waited the entire fifteen minutes to call him back. Once again the excitement in his voice gave me hope. "I spoke to the CEO of the hospital, and I told him your story. He was very touched and wanted to offer you a huge discount. He has never done this before; he has offered to give you a 65 percent discount. That would bring your amount to $28,000."

The amount sounded manageable. This would be a lot easier to make payments on than the other amount that was hanging over our heads. With confidence I thanked him for his efforts in assisting us and asked what kind of a payment plan could be established. But he said that in order to get this amazing deal, we would have to pay the total sum in thirty days. Needless to say, the feelings of hope dissipated quickly. But I asked him to keep the discount documented in the paperwork.

Once again I phoned Greg to tell him of the great, not-so-great news. He reminded me that our house in Austin had been on the market for several weeks without an offer. He figured that, were it to sell now, our equity would cover the bill.

But our discouragement grew with each passing day, as we had no new calls about the house. Three days before the deadline that would make the hospital bill revert to its initial $81,000, Greg was at the kitchen sink doing the dishes. He had a one-way conversation with God. "If you want us to continue this work, we need your help. You have to sell our house!" That afternoon we received two offers.

Yes, God continued to provide—maybe testing our faith in him to strengthen us to follow through with this calling. As I look back, I see the many times that it would have been so easy to give up and just do something else. But one of us has always had the fortitude to remind the other why we were doing this mission in the first place. This is part of what it means to be helpmates to each other. It's hard to believe how simple God's solutions are when the problems appear to be so complicated.

Greg

I remember one couple in particular: They had been married for eighteen years, and they'd been in counseling every year of their marriage. They came to us for three sessions, and when they came to the third session, the husband said, "I'm sorry; I'm a little mad."

"Why?" I asked. I thought for a moment we had done something wrong.

But he said, "My wife and I have been in counseling for eighteen years, and we've come to you guys for three sessions, and in three sessions we've learned more about life, more about our marriage, and more about our faith than in all those eighteen years of counseling. In *three sessions.* I hope you don't take offense about it, but what you have to offer is *simple.*"

"That's not offensive," I answered. "I take that as a compliment. A priest I know always says, 'When things become complicated, it's evidence of human involvement.' With God it is simple."

We've learned a lot since we started coaching. But probably the most important thing we've seen is that putting God first is the one thing everyone who comes to us needs. These couples all have different stories. They've all done different things. They all come from different backgrounds. And they all need the grace of God to get their marriages out of the trouble they're in.

We have three questions that couples must answer when they work with us—the three questions you saw at the beginning of the book:

1. *Is this marriage relationship something you want, and is it something you're willing to work on, and will you do the things we prescribe for you to do?*

If both husband and wife don't say yes, then we don't work with them. We tell them it would be a waste of our time and their time if they're not serious in going through this.

2. *Do you have the faith that Jesus Christ has the ability and the power to redeem your marriage and restore it to where it needs to be?*

This one is critically important. Look at all the accounts in the Bible of the miracles Christ performed. You'll see that there's no question of his ability to perform them. I mean, he's the God-man. He can do anything! But the miracle always comes about *with* the faith of the individual being healed.

> Take heart, daughter; your faith has made you well. (Matthew 9:22, emphasis added)

> O woman, great is your faith! Be it done for you as you desire. (Matthew 15:28, emphasis added)

> Your faith has saved you; go in peace. (Luke 7:50, emphasis added)

Receive your sight; your faith has made you well. (Luke 18:42, emphasis added)

All these accounts show us that we must be moved to the point where there's no shadow of a doubt that Christ has that ability, because that's where the power comes from. We have to believe that.

3. Do you give God permission to come into your life and redeem it?

God has given us free will, and he respects it so much that he would not violate that free will. So whatever we choose to do with it, he will honor our choice.

I'm an old basketball player, so this is the example I use: God's like the sixth man in a basketball game. The starting five are on the court, and it's the fourth period, with two minutes left. You're down by ten points, and God is that player who could not only come into that game and tie you up but also win the game for you. But the player is going to sit on that bench until the coach calls him into the game.

God is that player—and *you're* that coach. You've got to call him into the game. You've got to let him know that you want him to go to work.

When we meet with a couple, we meet once a week for the first three weeks, and then we take a break. Then we'll come back and reevaluate and see where we need to go from there. On average, we're finished coaching a couple in four or five sessions.

We don't want them to depend on us. We tell them this: "Our intention is to get you to a point where you can coach each other. Our information will not only give you an intellectual understanding of God's plan and design for marriage but also give you practical things to do in your marriage every day."

Of course, we really emphasize the sacraments—especially the sacrament of reconciliation, because the people who come to us need that one the most. It's your participation with God in the sacrament that makes you available for the grace. You don't just get that grace as a premium because you receive the sacrament. You have to work at it.

Remember that God has to be number one in your lives, because he's the source of the grace for you to meet each other's needs. We work out the priorities for people who come to us as follows: God is number one, and our spouse is number two. Our kids are number three, and after that come family and friends and everything else.

It's a kind of hierarchy that defines how a family needs to work if it's going to be what God intended it to be. A couple, with God's help, maintain a good marriage. Then they can assume their roles as the primary educators of their children, teaching them the ways of God and his Church.

Sometimes when I'm talking to couples, I'll take out a copy of the marital rite, and I'll tell them, "Look, if you got married in the Catholic Church, the priest or deacon used this marital rite. He asked you this series of questions, and the third question has two parts. The first part asks if you will openly accept children in this marriage relationship, and the second part asks if you will teach them the ways of the Lord and his Church.

"So if you as a married couple have kids, you have a duty and responsibility to teach them the ways of God and his Church. When you die and you see God face to face, you're going to be held responsible for how well or how poorly you did that job.

"You can look at it this way: as a couple, you provide the marriage preparation for your children. What you do and how you treat each other—your kids are just sitting around like little tape recorders taking it all in. When they grow up and press 'play,' they're going to replay and live out what they've seen you do in the course of your marriage relationship. You can *tell* your children whatever you like, but they're much more

to imitate what they see you doing."

What do your children see? Do they see a mom and dad who love and support each other faithfully (in both senses of the word *faith*)? Do they feel secure, knowing that their parents trust God for everything? Do they think that marriage is one of God's best inventions?

Do you think so?

Before you go on...
- In what areas of your married life have you had to trust God?
- In what areas do you still struggle to trust him?
- What are you teaching your children? Think about it for a moment.
- When was the last time your children saw you arguing with your spouse? What was the argument about? What do you think your children learned from what they saw? Is that what you want them to learn?

Afterword

THINGS ONCE LOOKED PRETTY DISMAL for us in our marriage, but look at us now. Whatever you've been through, we have probably done even worse things to each other. But we're more in love with each other now than we've ever been in our lives. Every day when we wake up, we can't wait to see each other.

That's what your marriage can be like. You really can have hope, regardless of what you're going through right now. And if you have a good marriage, it can be even better.

Are you ready to do the work it will take to get there?

We think you are. We think you *can* do it and that you *will* do it.

Just remember to keep praying, take responsibility for your own actions, and follow Christ's model: "I came to serve not to be served" (see Matthew 20:28; Mark 10:45). Then your marriage can be as amazing as ours. And we couldn't wish you anything better than that!

ABOUT THE AUTHORS

GREG AND JULIE ALEXANDER are the founders of The Alexander House, a nonprofit apostolate dedicated to the education and enrichment of marriage and family life. Their breakthrough work in marriage has been featured on EWTN, talk radio, and many publications, including Patrick Madrid's *Surprised by Truth 3, Envoy, Catholic Herald, Denver Catholic Register,* and *Our Sunday Visitor.* The Alexanders serve on the pastoral implementation committee for the USCCB Marriage Initiative, are members of the National Association of Catholic Family Life Ministers, and are trained marriage coaches. Greg and Julie have been married for over twenty years and have seven children.